LIFE ON THE HOME FRONT

LIFE ON THE HOME FRONT

Reader's Digest

Published by

THE READER'S DIGEST ASSOCIATION LIMITED

London   New York   Sydney   Montreal

LEND A HAND Every available opportunity was taken to support the war effort!

WAR CHILDREN Innocent victims of the war stare longingly from a Soviet concentration camp.

THREAT OF WAR Mother Russia is warned of the approaching Nazi menace.

HOME DEFENCE A poster calls upon the German people to fight for freedom and life.

LIFE ON THE HOME FRONT
Edited and designed by Toucan Books Limited
Sole author: Tim Healey

First edition copyright © 1993
The Reader's Digest Association Limited,
11 Westferry Circus, Canary Wharf, London E14 4HE

We are committed to both the quality of our products and the service we provide to our customers. We value your comments, so please feel free to contact us on 08705 113366, or via our Web site at www.readersdigest.co.uk
If you have any comments about the content of our books, you can contact us at gbeditorial@readersdigest.co.uk

Reprinted 2001

Copyright © 1993 Reader's Digest (Australia) Pty Ltd
Copyright © 1993 Reader's Digest Association Far East Limited
Philippines copyright © 1993
Reader's Digest Association Far East Limited

Separations: J Film Process Limited, Bangkok, Thailand

ISBN 0 276 42120 5

Front cover: (centre) GIs in London; (clockwise from top left) British evacuee; ARP badge; cigarette card; US Save Waste poster; tinned dried milk; German Home Defence poster.
Back cover: (centre) GI with London children; (clockwise from top left) song score; US cigarettes; Leningrad under seige; Parisian refugees; British identity card.

Page 1: Women welders break for a chat at the Bethlehem Steel shipyard.
Pages 2-3: A terrified child is rescued from a building in Buckingham Gate, London, after it was wrecked by a doodlebug in June 1944.

BOMBED LIBRARY Book lovers browse happily in the ruins of Holland House in Kensington, London.

SPIRIT OF RUSSIA A woman appeals to her compatriots to rise and avenge the destruction of her country.

CONTENTS

TIME OUT
Soldiers are encouraged to pause
at their friendly soda fountain.

BERLIN RUINS
A shattered city
on the brink of
defeat on
May 2, 1945.

MASTER PLAN
A German board
game details the
assault and capture
of the British Isles.

AVIS

La population est informée que
pour chaque soldat allemand qui
sera tué, 50 HOMMES SERONT
FUSILLES sur la Place de la Mairie.
L'interdiction de circulation est levée
ce jour, à partir de douze heures.
*Montreuil, le 19 Août 1944
LA MUNICIPALITE.

FRENCHMEN BEWARE!
Fifty of you will die
for every German
soldier killed.

NUCLEAR FALL-OUT   Irradiated
victims barely survive the
American atomic assault on Japan.

COUNTDOWN TO CONFLICT

'Peace in our time,' was the hope of British premier, Neville Chamberlain,

and of millions of other people worldwide. But dark clouds had long been gathering over Europe –

and the storm broke with Hitler's onslaught on Poland.

SHORTLY BEFORE 5am on Friday September 1, 1939, German forces stormed the Polish frontier. Tanks and motorised troops raced into the country over ground baked hard by a glorious summer. Supported by screeching Stuka dive-bombers, a total of 1.25 million men swept into Poland – and nothing could halt their advance. The world learned that day of a new and devastating tactic, known as the *Blitzkrieg* or 'lightning war'.

Berlin radio carried a threatening proclamation by Hitler as early as 5.33 that morning, but many Germans first heard of the invasion at breakfast. It was a beautiful morning, with a tinge of autumn in the air. Loudspeaker vans decked with swastikas roared through towns: '*Achtung! Achtung!* In the early hours of this morning the Führer's troops have invaded Poland. Germany is at war!' The national anthem and the *Horst Wessel* song (the Nazi Party hymn) followed, at full volume. Families ran out onto the pavements. Schoolgirl Renate Ungewitter saw them lingering dazed and silent in front of their houses after a loud-speaker van moved on. 'Shocked, everybody stood for a while and then they went on with what they had been doing.'

Later on that Friday morning Hitler addressed the Reichstag in Berlin, informing the assembly of the recent events.

The capital's foreign correspondents were all there, and short-wave radio crackled out a simultaneous commentary upon his speech around the world. Feverish diplomatic activity followed these events, and it was only when all ultimatums had failed that Britain declared war on Germany.

At 11am on September 3, British listeners tuned in to the BBC to hear an announcement to stand by for a speech by the Prime Minister, Neville Chamberlain. All over the nation families gathered around their sets. 'While we were waiting, I glanced out of the window,' a woman recalls. 'There wasn't a soul in sight or a vehicle, there was just this lone cat stalking across the road.' At 11.15am, following a programme in which a lady was giving a talk about tinned-food recipes, Neville Chamberlain came on the air. His voice was tired and strained. Britain had called for an undertaking from Hitler to withdraw his troops from Poland. 'I have to tell you now that no such under-taking has been received and that consequently this country is at war with Germany.'

Only a few minutes later, sirens wailed out all over London and many other parts of the country, as far north as Sheffield. People

SIEG HEIL Hitler addresses a pre-war rally. Above: the Führer's troops enter Prague in 1939 to be greeted with enthusiasm by some German residents of the Czech capital.

SINISTER BOUQUET   A young girl presents a bunch of flowers to Hitler before the outbreak of the war.

hurried to their air-raid shelters. Then the All Clear sounded – it had been a false alarm, triggered by a friendly plane carrying two French officers across the south coast. An eerie relaxation spread. The situation was accepted soberly: there were no outbreaks of flag-waving hysteria as there had been at the start of World War I.

The British dominions, Australia and New Zealand also joined the struggle on September 3. So too did France, whose government declared war at 5pm. French men and women listened tensely to the announcement, for their eastern border directly adjoined Hitler's bullying Reich and there was much nervous talk in the Parisian cafés. Indeed, throughout Europe, even nations not yet involved in the conflict became anxious. Sweden and Norway, determined to remain neutral, nevertheless put their armed forces on red alert.

There followed an edgy seven-month period known in Britain as the Bore War or Phoney War, in France as the *drôle de guerre* (funny war) and in Germany as the *Sitzkrieg* (armchair war). Though nations were geared up for mass confrontations, nobody seemed in a hurry to start fighting on land.

The long overture ended, however, with a terrible crescendo in the spring and summer of 1940, as first Denmark, and then Norway, the Low Countries and France all fell to a new wave of Nazi onslaughts.

Mussolini's Italy entered the conflict on June 10, 1940, while the Germans surged towards Paris. Persuaded by Hitler's success that he must wait no longer, the hesitant Mussolini took his nation into the drama with no great confidence. That night, an aura of gloom hung over Rome. A dejected *Times* correspondent passing down Corso Umberto and across the Piazza di Spagna saw not one flag hung out. 'I feel miserable,' Count Ciano, the foreign minister, wrote in his diary. 'The adventure begins. May God help Italy!'

Stalin's Russia had started the war as a partner of Germany, by the terms of the notorious Nazi-Soviet pact, but shortly before dawn on June 22, 1941, Hitler launched a surprise attack, codenamed Operation Barbarossa, on his former collaborator. That Sunday morning, Radio Moscow came on air with its usual fare of physical-fitness drill and children's programmes. The streets of the capital gradually filled with sightseers and shoppers (Sunday was the main shopping day in Moscow) and it was midday before news of the invasion broke. By then, the German army was sweeping eastward along a thousand-mile front, leaving towns devastated and airfields littered with burning planes. Stalin would not speak to the nation that day – he locked himself into his office – and it was left to the foreign minister,

SEPTEMBER 1939 Newspaper readers in London learn of the German attack on Poland.

POLAND INVADED
Several Towns Bombed
HITLER LAUNCHES FULL SCALE ATTACK
"Danzig Annexed"
BRITISH PARLIAMENT MEET TONIGHT

HITLER TELLS ITALY "WE WILL CARRY OUT OUR TASK ALONE"

JUNE 1941   Anxious Moscow residents hear the public announcements of the Nazi invasion of Russia.

Molotov, to address the people, broadcasting through loudspeakers that boomed from every street corner in the capital: 'The Government calls upon you, men and women of the Soviet Union, to rally round the glorious Bolshevik Party and its great leader, Comrade Stalin. Our cause is just. The enemy will be beaten.'

War was to come to the United States with similar suddenness. *'Tora! Tora! Tora!'* (Tiger! Tiger! Tiger!) was the signal that went out as Japanese torpedo bombers screamed down on the American warships crowding the naval base at Pearl Harbor, Hawaii. The surprise attack began at 7.55am on the morning of Sunday December 7, 1941. Seven battleships were sunk or put out of action in the two-hour maelstrom of bombs, billowing smoke and raking machine-gun fire. Over 2400 people were left dead or missing. In the United States itself, news of the attack hit the airwaves that afternoon. In a Dallas cinema where news of the bombing interrupted a Gary Cooper film, *Time* magazine reported: 'There was a pause, a pinpoint of silence, a prolonged sigh, and then thundering applause. A steelworker said, "We'll kick their teeth in!"' In New York a radio station interrupted coverage of a Giants-Dodgers football game – angry, unbelieving calls quickly jammed its switchboard. On the West Coast, the onslaught triggered real fear of a Japanese invasion: the mayor of San Francisco declared a state of emergency, while the governor of California called out the National Guard. Thousands of Americans were already storming the recruiting offices by 1pm the next day, when President Roosevelt asked Congress to declare war on Japan. The day of Pearl Harbor, he declared, was 'a date that will live in infamy'.

In Tokyo, however, the attack was seen as a dazzling Japanese initiative which had ended months of diplomatic tension. Celebrations broke out in the capital – though the mood of jubilation was tempered by some fears of an immediate retaliation. Saito Mutsuo, a schoolboy at the time, remembers: 'Our first thought after we heard the news was that the Americans might start to bomb us right away. So I didn't go in to the crammer that day – I went down to the nearest corner store and bought some strong rice paper and a pot of glue. It probably sounds rather silly now, but I spent the whole of the morning of the day that war broke out going round the house covering the windows with sheets of paper to protect us from flying glass.'

Blackout precautions, wailing sirens, bombing and evacuation were realities known to millions of people in many different nations in World War II. And even in countries which saw minimal damage done on their own soil, the organisation of the home front transformed society. The mobilisation of women for industry, the rationing of food and clothing, the morale-boosting films and newsreels, the packing of parcels, the homecomings and the harrowing tragedies, all combined to make the global drama a uniquely powerful experience for all who lived through it.

"I am looking forward to dictating peace to the United States in the White House at Washington"
— ADMIRAL YAMAMOTO

What do YOU say, AMERICA?

ENTER AMERICA A poster attacks the architect of the Pearl Harbor attack. Right: a newsboy proclaims that war is on.

BRITAIN SEES IT THROUGH

On September 3, 1939, the Sunday-morning sound of hand-pushed

lawnmowers came to a stop in Britain as people clustered around their wireless

sets to hear the news that the country was at war.

Within seconds, the first air-raid warning rang out:

a foretaste of the future in which German bombers, such as the Heinkel III above,

dropped daily terror from the skies.

BRITAIN PREPARES

'You must not be taken by surprise', warned a Ministry of Information leaflet issued as the threat of invasion loomed in Britain. Long before war broke out families were introduced to gas masks, air-raid drill and bomb shelters, and mass evacuations were planned.

IN BRITAIN, preparations for the possibility of mass bombing had begun long before the war broke out. By the end of September 1938 some 38 million gas masks had been given out, house to house, to British families. They were never to be needed. Yet these cumbersome items loomed large in everyday life during the early stages of the war. They were carried in square cardboard cartons under the arm, or slung in knapsacks over the shoulder. Fitted onto the head they made breathing difficult and smelt of rubber and disinfectant. Children discovered, to their delight, that you could blow rude noises by exhaling sharply into them so that their clammy side pieces vibrated against the cheeks.

The steel-built, tunnel-shaped Anderson shelter, erected in people's gardens, proved more valuable. In February 1939 the Home Office – the government department responsible for law and order and people's safety – announced plans to distribute shelters to thousands of homes in the areas most likely to be hit; the shelters took their name from Sir John Anderson, the Lord Privy Seal in charge of air-raid precautions. About 2 million shelters had been issued by September 1939. Made from six curved sheets bolted together at the top, with steel plates at either end, and measuring 6ft 6in by 4ft 6in (1.95m by 1.35m), the Anderson shelters could accommodate six people, or more if bunks were suitably arranged. A shelter could

SIGNS OF THE TIMES After the fall of France, street names and signposts were dismantled to confuse any invading Germans (left). As early as spring 1939, corrugated steel Anderson shelters were being delivered to these homes in a north London suburb (above). They proved damp and prone to flooding – but they did save lives.

GAS ALERT During the early weeks of the war, daily life in offices, shops, schools and factories was often disturbed by gas-mask drills. Hitler never made a gas attack, however.

SELF-PROTECTION The public was deluged with official leaflets giving advice on personal and home protection.

be erected by two people without experience, and was half buried in the ground with earth heaped on top.

Leaflets about home defence were pushed through letter-boxes during the summer of 1939, advising on how a cellar or basement might be converted into a refuge room, and how sandbags might be stacked to protect against bomb blast. There was guidance on

blackout restrictions, too, that sent people scurrying out to buy thick curtains, blackout paint, cardboard, brown paper and drawing pins – all to blot out the least glimmer of light from windows in case it should help enemy bombers.

The blackout proper began on the night of September 1, 1939, when all street lights were turned

THE YOUNG PRINCESSES AT WAR

IN SEPTEMBER 1940, when bombs struck Buckingham Palace, a policeman observed to the Queen: 'A magnificent piece of bombing, Ma'am, if you'll pardon my saying so.' The sense that the Royal Family was sharing in the dangers of other Londoners did much to cement bonds of loyalty. People were fascinated by such facts as the baths in Buckingham Palace having a 5in (13cm) watermark on them, to help save water and fuel.

During the war's early months Princess Elizabeth and her sister Princess Margaret Rose were sent to Balmoral in Scotland. But later, despite the danger from bombs, to

keep the family together they returned to Royal Lodge, Windsor, sometimes staying at Windsor

Castle, too. It was from the castle that the 14-year-old Princess Elizabeth made her radio debut on October 13, 1940, in a broadcast to evacuee children. In April 1942, at the age of 16, Princess Elizabeth registered for war service and in March 1945, despite opposition from her family and the War Cabinet, she trained as a driver in the Auxiliary Territorial Service (ATS), where she was to hold the rank of a second lieutenant.

ROYAL SOLDIER Princess Elizabeth joined the Auxiliary Territorial Service in 1945. There she learned to drive and maintain Army motor vehicles.

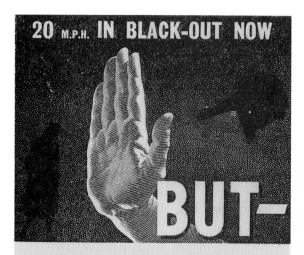

20 M.P.H. IN BLACK-OUT NOW

BUT—

YOU CAN STILL SEE CARS LONG BEFORE DRIVERS SEE YOU!

..and still The Railways carry on!

LIGHTS OUT The blackout began on September 1, 1939. Speed restrictions came into force and white lines were painted on kerbs and lampposts to help motorists and pedestrians. Although trains kept running, they were slow and crowded, their carriages lit (if at all) only by dim blue pin-points of light.

off and cars crawled along roads with their headlights extinguished. The results were alarming. Pedestrians tripped over kerbstones, twisted ankles, or crashed into one another on the pavement. In that first September the number of road accidents soared, and the total killed on the road almost doubled.

In 1939 there were already 1.5 million people involved in civil defence, including air-raid wardens, ambulance drivers, first-aid helpers and fire fighters. More than two-thirds of them were volunteers recruited in their local boroughs and amongst the

COVER UP Gun emplacements, factories and airfields were all disguised by the use of camouflage netting. This painting is by the prolific war artist Mary Dunbar.

most conspicuous were the ARP (Air Raid Precautions) wardens, kitted out in tin helmets and blue overalls. The WVS (Women's Voluntary Service) was an organisation whose members staffed field kitchens, rest centres, hostels and nurseries.

Municipal shelters were built of brick and concrete, and trench shelters were dug in parks. While these precautions were being taken, city authorities were quietly estimating the number of cardboard coffins that would be needed after an air attack. City skies were transformed by the appearance of huge silver barrage balloons, floating like shoals of friendly whales over rooftops. Each was moored by its hawser to a wagon with a winch on its back. Their cables were designed to stop low flights and pinpoint bombing by enemy aircraft, and many people found them a reassuring presence. Sometimes, though, in bad weather a balloon had to be cut free and would go wildly out of control, trailing wires that smashed chimney-pots, damaged roofs or cut trolley-bus cables.

There were more precautions still. The Registrar General proclaimed that everyone was to have an identity card and number in the event of war. On the Saturday before war began, pictures from the National Gallery left London to be stored for safety in a quarry in Wales. Hundreds of thousands of people streamed out of the cities for the safety of friends' houses or country hotels in the West Country and Scotland. And on 1 September, as Hitler's troops crossed into Poland, the official evacuation began.

THE EVACUEES

All kinds of people were regarded by the Government as suitable for evacuation to relative safety outside the big towns and cities. They included about 25,000 civil servants and their documents. But children, above all, were thought to need protection. No one was compelled to go, but the authorities offered plenty of encouragement and in September 1939 the number of official evacuees was about 1 million.

It was an epic undertaking, long planned with practice marches out of the school gates. On the first morning of the exodus, journalists reported a strange quietness in the streets as vast armies of youngsters passed by, labelled and clutching their gas masks,

heading for the buses that would carry them to the main-line stations. After their train journey they arrived at an often unknown destination tired, hungry and uncertain whether they would ever see their families again. On arrival there were 'pick-your-evacuee' sessions where hosts haggled over the most presentable children while the sicklier and grubbier were left until last. Evacuees were billeted on people – if you had spare room you had to take them in. Complaints of thieving, swearing, bed-wetting and general smelliness were made time and again against the 'townie' children who came in disproportionate numbers from the slums and backstreets of Britain's big cities.

Genteel spinsters and quiet bachelors were expected to cope with streetwise urchins suffering, perhaps, from scabies or impetigo. The children's sanitary habits were alarming. A Glasgow mother, evacuated with her six-year-old, was reported to

COUNTRY LIFE When schoolchildren were evacuated from city to countryside their teachers went too, and classes were sometimes held out of doors. It was all very new to many town children. 'They call this spring, Mum, and they have one down here every year', one evacuee wrote. A Chelsea schoolboy (right) prepares to leave London, carrying his gas mask.

"Let 'em all come"

MEN
41-55

HOME DEFENCE
BATTALIONS
Apply at any Army Recruiting Centre Now

DAD'S ARMY The Local Defence Volunteers, or Home Guard, were recruited to resist invasion. The park-keeper volunteers (above) were lucky to have rifles for inspection. In the early days many drilled with sporting guns, clubs or broom handles. By 1942 the Home Guard was being taken more seriously.

exclaim: 'You dirty thing, messing up the lady's carpet. Go and do it in the corner.' (In tenements lacking decent sanitation it was sometimes still the habit to urinate on newspaper indoors.) Small wonder that there was friction, with hosts paid only a meagre sum for a child's board and lodging.

The city-bred children were often homesick and disorientated. Many had never seen green fields or cows before. Knives and forks were a novelty. Underwear was greeted with incomprehension. Some later remembered their experience with fondness, recalling kindly hosts, the pleasures of blackberry-picking expeditions, stealing apples from orchards and other country delights. But the episode was generally a failure. All through the autumn of the so-called Phoney War, when no bombs fell to justify the exodus, the evacuees trickled back to the towns.

THE HOME GUARD

For months after the outbreak of war, the expected swarms of German bombers failed to appear over British cities. This strange, edgy period known as the Phoney War lasted well into 1940, but the evacuation of the British army from the Channel port of Dunkirk

and the fall of France prompted real fears of invasion. In May 1940 War Minister Anthony Eden called for a new defence force to be set up. It was originally known as the LDV (Local Defence Volunteers): recruits were supposed to be between 17 and 65 years of age and the only fitness requirement was that they should be 'capable of free movement'. The response was immense. A quarter of a million men joined within a week and the numbers had doubled by July when, at Churchill's suggestion, the force was renamed the Home Guard.

The volunteers were not paid and, in the early days, few were equipped with rifles; one gun had to serve for ten men on average. Whiskery old veterans of World War I, and earlier, paraded alongside beardless boys, drilling with sporting guns, walking sticks, golf clubs, broom handles – whatever was available. The Home Guard's task was to keep watch on coasts, public buildings, roads, railways and so on for signs of enemy invaders, who might come by parachute as well as in seaborne landings. Home Guard members also did important work in bringing in enemy airmen who had been forced to bale out of wrecked aircraft.

MASS BOMBING

For nearly a year, between summer 1940 and spring 1941, the British were subjected to a sustained aerial assault. Gradually, however, people got used to the daily ordeal of bombing and, after a night spent huddled in a subterranean air-raid shelter, it was back to work and business as usual.

THE WAIL of the air-raid sirens ... the drone of enemy aircraft overhead ... the WHAM WHAM of the anti-aircraft batteries ... the crump of the bombs ... these were the Blitz's sombre sound-effects. Britons endured their first civilian bomb casualties in March 1940 as the German Luftwaffe attacked the huge Scapa Flow naval base, in the extreme north of Scotland. Larger bombing raids were mounted from July, at the outset of the Battle of Britain. But it was not until summer's end that the Blitz proper began – a sustained aerial assault on selected cities, ports and industrial centres that lasted until May 1941. London, Birmingham, Bristol, Glasgow, Coventry, Manchester and Liverpool were among the key targets. Raids were made on the same areas for several nights running, to bring infernos of flames, smashed brickwork, splintered glass and black, asphyxiating smoke. In the chaos, entire streets simply vanished, burying mothers, fathers and children in the rubble.

Nearly 2000 people were killed or wounded in London's first night of the Blitz, Saturday, September 7,

1940. The brunt of the attack was borne by the East End where the docks were the important targets. Watching from central London, air-raid warden Barbara Nixon saw fire engines racing eastward, clanging their bells. A vast pink cloud turned angry red and blackened around the edges. 'From our vantage point it was remote and, from a spectacular point of view, beautiful. One had to force oneself to picture the misery and the havoc below in the most overcrowded area of London.'

At ground level the East End's experience was eerily horrific. Len Jones, a teenager at the time, recalled the whole of King Street rising and falling, with shrapnel dancing off the cobbles: '... the suction and compression from the high-explosive blasts just pulled and pushed you ... you could actually feel your eyeballs being sucked out ... ' Bomb blast, people would learn, had weird effects: it could rip victims limb from limb, or leave them unharmed but stripped naked.

On that first night in London the German planes kept on coming in waves, lured by a Thames aglow

---

THE NIGHT WE WENT THROUGH HELL

BRISTOL, NOVEMBER 24, 1940

❛ Jerry is here early tonight. Siren went five minutes ago. Yes, he's here all right. Some bombs are being dropped and a fire has started already to the east of us. I've got a nasty feeling in my tummy too at this moment. God grant it is going to be all right for us. 11.05pm same night: we've been through hell.

Never have I experienced anything like it. Tummy still wobbly. Fires and bombs everywhere. Went to the cellar at first, but couldn't settle down, so went to the sitting-room. We didn't need any light for the room was lit up with the glare of the fires. Wine Street looks as if it is no more. Fires all seemed centred in

that direction, though up the hill at the back of our place there are fires also. One looks like Princes Theatre. Our sitting-room-window woodwork is so hot you can hardly bear your hand on it. The house rocks as the bombs drop. ❜

From the diary of a Bristol woman.

MIRACLE ESCAPE   During three weeks in September 1940 about 10,000 high-explosive bombs were dropped on the London region. On October 10, St Paul's Cathedral received a direct hit but the bomb destroyed only the high altar.

DAILY HERALD

No. 7725
EXTRA LATE EDITION
SATURDAY, NOVEMBER 16, 1940
ONE PENNY

Midlands City Is Now Like A Bombarded French Town

COVENTRY HOMELESS SLEPT BY ROADSIDE THIS MORNING

NOT A MORTAL BLOW —WORK WILL RESTART

By F. G. H. SALUSBURY, "Daily Herald" War Correspondent

COVENTRY, Friday Night

COVENTRY HAS BEEN THE VICTIM OF THE MOST CONCENTRATED, IF NOT THE WORST, RAID SINCE THE WAR BEGAN.

I HAVE JUST COME BACK FROM THE CENTRE OF THE CITY, WHICH NOW LOOKS EXACTLY LIKE ONE OF THOSE FRENCH TOWNS THAT WERE LAID LEVEL DURING THE LAST WAR BY AN INTENSIVE BOMBARDMENT.

The cathedral is in ruins, except for its tower, and over a large area surrounding it there lies the stench of burning houses.

The number of casualties cannot yet be determined, but it is certainly large. (Preliminary reports, says the Ministry of Home Security, indicate that the number of casualties may number 1,000.) The damage which has been inflicted on this city must run into millions of pounds.

I was told by one of the inhabitants that the noise of falling bombs was practically continuous, and that after a short time everyone was literally dazed by the noise.

I approached the city from Rugby, and a few miles out of Coventry I encountered the first huge body of refugee walking along the roadside exactly as the Belgians and French escaped from the last German invasion.

Children were being carried in their fathers' arms, and pushed along in perambulators. Luggage was piled high in perambulators.

Three famous spires of Coventry—Christ Church, Holy Trinity Church and the Cathedral.

RAF STRIKES AT BERLIN

WHILE the Germans were concentrating their hate on Coventry, R.A.F bombers were pounding the great Berlin railway stations and goods yards.

Heavy explosive and incendiary bombs caused fires that could be seen for many miles. The damage will increase the transport chaos in Germany already caused by the R.A.F. (See Page Six.)

21 Down—Three In Last Night's Raid

AFTER a day in which eighteen German bombers and fighters were shot down in raids on Britain—for the loss of one Spitfire and one pilot—London had its worst night blitz for several weeks.

Three more enemy planes were destroyed in the night raids.

London anti-aircraft guns put up the fiercest barrage for weeks when relays of raiders attacked the capital in the early hours this morning.

Raids were widespread over the country. The West Midlands were again bombed, and several towns in the Home Counties.

But London appeared to be the host of the main attack.

During the first few hours of the night only single bombers came.

Dusk To Dawn Raid

NAZIS SAY 30,000 FIRE BOMBS FELL

FROM dusk on Thursday to light explosives, rendered important their efforts to save the night only single bombers came.

STOP PRESS

BERLIN RAIDED AGAIN

NEW YORK, Friday

German broadcast intercepted by National Broadcasting Company said large numbers of British planes attacked Berlin to-night, and six were brought down in Berlin, and six near the Channel.

BRITAIN'S OFFER TO RUSSIA

GREAT BRITAIN is still awaiting Moscow's reply to the proposals made to Russia last month.

There were three main items in the proposals it was learned in London last night. They were:

The facto recognition of the incorporation of the Baltic States in the Soviet Union.

A guarantee that Russia would be a participant in any peace settlement after the war; and

An assurance that Britain would not be assaulted in any attack against Soviet Russia.

The proposals were submitted to M. Vishinsky, the deputy Commissar for Foreign Affairs, on October 22.

AN ITALIAN LIE

The Admiralty last night gave the truth to an Italian claim to have sunk the battleship of the Ramillies class.

THE MORNING AFTER Firemen sift through the rubble in Coventry after the massive raid of November 1940. The city's 14th-century cathedral was destroyed and more than 1000 citizens were either killed or seriously injured.

with blazing barges and flames reflected from the wharves. At Surrey Docks on the southern bank the heat was so intense that it blistered the paintwork of the fireboats on the opposite side of the river, and solid embers the size of footballs whirled away to start fresh fires elsewhere. Warehouses spilled blazing rum into the streets, causing paint drums to explode, and also spewed melting rubber that billowed with inky, noxious fumes, while flaming sugar flowed in cataracts over the dockside to form fiery sheets on the water's surface. For the following 56 nights, London was to be bombed from dusk to dawn.

Nor was London alone. The populations of the other great ports and cities knew similar terrors, and Coventry was subjected to a night of such annihilating ferocity that the Germans coined a new word: *Coventrieren,* to Coventrate. Wherever the bombs fell every-day life was violently disrupted. Mrs M. Price was a young bride working in the Midlands: 'The first morning I went in there was a bomb in the workshop. Another morning, on arriving in the centre of Birmingham to catch the tram, there were 18 fires blazing around us at the same time. Water from the fire hoses was flooding everywhere and fur coats were being swilled down the street.' Cuthbert Douse recalls helping to dig his grandmother out of a house in the Glasgow area: 'We had to dig with our hands but her arm was jammed by the windowsill. I remember my father telling me to turn away because the only way to get her out was to pull. I'm afraid he pulled three of her fingers off getting her out of the debris.'

Even country districts suffered. The county of Kent, south-east of the capital, was known as 'bomb alley' because it lay on the flight path to London. People became used to the throb of enemy aircraft over quiet woods and villages and on one Kentish farm a single pasturage was scarred by 93 bomb holes – one of them 40ft (12.2m) across. The farmer's son said: 'As a

AIR-RAID WARDENS They supervised air-raid procedures in the streets and in shelters, issued gas masks and checked the blackout. One in every six was a woman.

19

THE LONDON UNDERGROUND AT WAR

WHEN THE BOMBS began to rain down on London, many people turned to the Underground system as a place of refuge. The Government was at first reluctant to allow the use of tube stations as shelters, partly because officials were worried that civilians might succumb to a 'deep shelter' mentality and vanish underground, giving up on the war effort. But there was nothing to prevent anyone buying a 1^1/2d ticket (the cheapest fare) and waiting out a raid.

People started going down as early as 11.30am to claim a pitch for the night. By the time of the five o'clock rush hour tube users had to step between rows of men, women and children who ate, drank, read the papers, fed their babies or slept in what one reporter has dubbed 'the most extraordinary mass picnic the world has ever known'.

To keep working platforms clear, transport officials painted two white lines, 4ft and 8ft (1.2m and 2.4m) respectively, from the platform's edge. Tube-dwellers were not supposed to cross the 8ft line before 7.30pm. Then the barrier was moved to the 4ft line until 10.30pm when the trains stopped running, the electric current was turned off and people

TUBE DWELLERS Sleeping Londoners crowd the platform of the Underground station at the Elephant and Castle, scene of a huge conflagration in 1941.

were even able to sleep on the track.

At the height of the Blitz the stations were sheltering 177,000 people every night in very unwholesome conditions. Mosquitoes and lice thrived among the huddled figures. Nor were the tube stations as safe as many believed. In the worst accident, at Balham, about 680 shelterers fell victim to a bomb that made a direct hit, burying many in the rubble.

break from bombing we sometimes get machine-gunning. That is definitely not so healthy. We had just left off threshing the other day when one blighter came hurtling down to 150ft and sprayed us. We threw ourselves under a wagon just in time.'

Sometimes German bombers made mistakes and dropped their bombs in entirely the wrong areas. At other times, returning from a raid, they would dump the remainder of their explosives at random in order to fly home with greater safety. Many bombs fell on suburbs. No one within any distance of a likely target could sleep entirely easy in their beds.

On September 13, 1940, Buckingham Palace itself

was bombed – an event that quickened feelings of solidarity among all classes. 'I'm glad we've been bombed,' was the Queen's famous remark. 'It makes me feel that I can look the East End in the face.'

TAKING COVER

The East End suffered the most. In the early days, thousands fled nightly to makeshift camps in the woodlands of Epping Forest, just north-east of the city; others took shelter in Chislehurst Caves, some ancient chalk tunnels south-east of London. Yet more found refuge in the Tilbury shelter, a subterranean goods yard in Stepney in the very heart of the East

BUSINESS AS USUAL Office workers in London, 1940, pick their way through the debris after a raid. To make up for lost sleep they took naps continually, even 'in the lift going up to my floor', one reported. From 1941 the Fire Guard (below) supervised street fire-fighting.

Beat 'FIREBOMB FRITZ'

BRITAIN SHALL NOT BURN

BRITAIN'S FIRE GUARD IS BRITAIN'S DEFENCE

End, where as many as 16,000 people huddled together in a seething mass and filthy conditions. People slept under railway arches. London's Underground stations were invaded by huge crowds seeking safety.

Gradually, though, people got used to the nightly ordeals of the bombings. Shops and offices closed early to allow the staff time to get home and make their arrangements before the sirens sounded. The next morning, with the scent of smoke and brick-dust still hanging in the air, the tired shop-girls and red-eyed clerks were back at work. Dazed families whose homes had been destroyed were cared for in so-called Rest Centres, sited in school buildings and church halls and staffed mostly by volunteers. Homeless, exhausted and sometimes in long-term shock, the dispossessed might stay there for weeks, having nowhere else to go. Still, for the mass of the people it was business as usual. 'Don't tell me. I've got a bomb story too', read a lapel badge widely worn at the time.

RISK AND REWARD

There was a sensation when a parachute bomb smashed through the roof of the London Palladium to dangle, still live, in the wings. It was a naval officer who defused it. He was rewarded with free tickets to the Palladium for life.

The Blitz on London entered its final phase in May 1941 with a raid that left a third of the capital's streets impassable and 155,000 families without gas, water or electricity. Thereafter the attacks eased off, but occasional raids continued to affect different parts of the country. In 1942 the Luftwaffe launched an offensive against Britain's historic cities, particularly Exeter, Bath, Norwich, York and Canterbury. They were nicknamed 'Baedeker raids' from the assumption that the famous tourist guidebooks had been consulted when the list of targets was drawn up. Though the damage was slight by the standards of the Blitz, the raids brought grief and concern to many families who had thought themselves safe from any danger of bombardment.

And in 1944, the population of London and the surrounding region would know new terrors in the form of V-1 and V-2 attacks.

THE HOME AT WAR

SANDBAGGED against bomb blast, with its taped and curtained windows, the average middle-class home took on a curiously secretive appearance in wartime Britain. At the outset of the war, when people feared poison-gas attacks, the government advised equipping a downstairs room as an indoor refuge, which was supposed to be carefully gas-proofed.

Steel-built Anderson shelters were available for the garden. During the Blitz many people never undressed at night but slept on their beds with their clothes on, ready to dash for the cold, damp Anderson shelter when the sirens went off – clutching vital family documents, personal treasures, pillows, blankets and sleeping bags.

After a harrowing experience, such as a hit or a near miss, the whole street would help out, neighbours hurrying round with cups of tea to soothe shattered nerves.

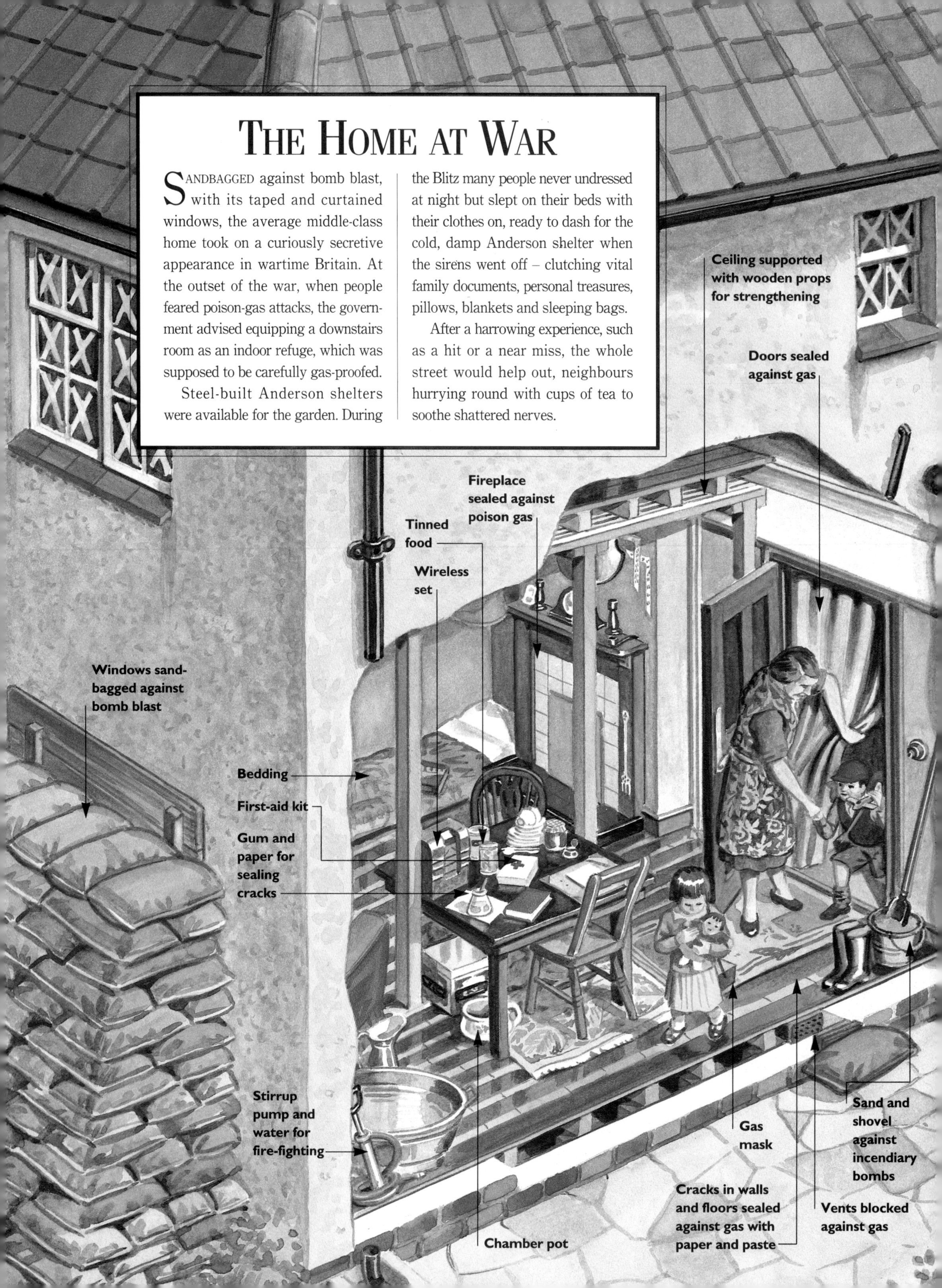

Ceiling supported with wooden props for strengthening

Doors sealed against gas

Fireplace sealed against poison gas

Tinned food

Wireless set

Windows sand-bagged against bomb blast

Bedding

First-aid kit

Gum and paper for sealing cracks

Stirrup pump and water for fire-fighting

Chamber pot

Gas mask

Cracks in walls and floors sealed against gas with paper and paste

Sand and shovel against incendiary bombs

Vents blocked against gas

Vegetables grown on shelter roof

Flowerpot heater (candle under an upturned flowerpot)

Oil lamp

Windows taped against damage from splintered glass. Blackout curtains inside

Doorway shielded by earth-filled soap boxes and pale-fencing

Bicycle headlamp masked for blackout

Victory garden

Anderson shelter

PIG FOOD

Railings removed for metal salvage

Food scraps collected as swill for pigs

Air-raid warden

Street lighting not used in wartime

MAKING DO

Beetroot juice for lipstick and winter coats fashioned from curtain material . . . flowerbeds dug up

to plant potatoes and chickens kept on the roof . . . all were routine in wartime Britain when

many essentials were either rationed or unobtainable and people had to 'make do'.

FOR MANY PEOPLE, the oddities and austerities of the daily diet are among the most vivid memories of civilian life in World War II. Food rationing was introduced to Britain in stages. A cautious beginning was made on January 8, 1940, with rationing on bacon and butter (4oz (115g) per person per week) and sugar (12oz (340g)). The law declared that every householder must register with their local shops. Meat rationing followed in March and was by price rather than weight. The cheaper the cut, the more was available. From July, tea, cooking fats, jam and cheese were rationed. For eggs and milk the Government used a different rationing system: supplies were allocated to shops in proportion to the number of customers registered there. People were permitted one egg per fortnight, though supplies were not guaranteed as they were with the other rationed goods. Additionally, a points system gave shoppers a choice of foods such as breakfast cereals, biscuits, canned fruit and fish. These were all valued at a certain number of points, and customers could buy what they wanted up to a maximum of points.

All in all it was a complicated system involving a lot of paperwork. But despite official misgivings, rationing proved popular with most people because of its fairness. The rich were hit as much as the poor. In the better-off houses, it was reported, a weekend guest might arrive with his own little parcel of butter to give to the butler who took his suitcase.

To ensure that everyone was adequately nourished,

FOOD CHAIN Queuing was a wartime institution. A million British women lined up every day for their groceries, often bringing newspaper because wrapping paper was in short supply. Official recipe leaflets (left) encouraged healthy eating.

Potato RECIPE SLIP **P.2**

CAKE MIXTURE WITH MASHED POTATO (for 4 persons)

1 dried egg, dry
6 oz. flour
Pinch of salt
2 level teaspoon baking powder
2 oz. fat
2 oz. mashed potato
1½ oz. sugar
Household milk to mix

Dried Egg RECIPE SLIP **D.E.6**

MEXICAN CREAM (for 4 persons)

2 level tablespoons dried egg
2 level tablespoons flour
2-4 level tablespoons cocoa
2-4 level tablespoons sugar
Pinch of salt
1 pint moderately strong coffee
Vanilla essence

METHOD.—Mix the dry ingredients together and mix to a smooth paste with a little coffee. Boil the remaining coffee. Pour on to the other ingredients, return to the pan and boil 2-3 minutes. Add vanilla and pour into individual glasses or a serving dish. Serve cold.

MEALS ON WHEELS A mobile canteen delivers food to a bomb-damaged London suburb. Mobile laundries and baths also offered relief when homes were destroyed or when supplies of gas, water and electricity were cut off.

what were called British Restaurants were set up, where workers could get a meal at a modest cost: minced beef with carrots and parsnips was a typical dish. To boost the vitamin intake, the Ministry of Health, made sure that every child received daily milk, cod liver oil and orange juice. The Ministry also filled newspapers with Food Facts designed to keep the nation healthy, and to make the best of unrestricted foods, particularly vegetables. Open any periodical, it seemed, and there was 'Good News About Carrots!'

MINISTRY OF FOOD RECIPES

War and Peace Pudding

❛ This pudding was made in Canada during the last war. Since then, many people have never bothered with a rich Christmas pudding.

Mix together one cupful of flour, one cupful of breadcrumbs, half a cupful of suet, half a cupful of mixed dried fruit, and, if you like, a teaspoon of mixed sweet spice. Then add a cupful of grated raw carrot and finally a level teaspoonful of bicarbonate of soda dissolved in two tablespoonfuls of hot water. Mix all together, turn into a well-greased pudding bowl. The bowl should be not more than two-thirds full. Boil or steam for at least two hours.

Carrot Croquettes

Six carrots, 1oz margarine, oatmeal, 1 gill of milk, 1oz cornflour, fat for frying, seasoning to taste.

Boil the carrots till tender, drain and put through a sieve. Add seasoning to taste. Make a thick white sauce with the cornflour, margarine and milk, and then add the sieved carrot to it. Leave till cold, then shape into croquettes, roll in oatmeal and fry in deep hot fat. Drain well and serve. ❜

Potato Pete's recipe book

EAT ME Doctor Carrot and Potato Pete were propaganda figures created to encourage consumption of available vegetables.

How to make
your Lux Toilet Soap
last longer

POINTS TO REMEMBER

ALWAYS keep your Lux Toilet Soap dry between usings. It's best to place it on a little rubber mat, if you have one, or in a wire tray.

NEVER let the soap lie about in the basin or bath while you're washing. Nothing will waste away your soap more quickly.

ALWAYS stick the remains of your soap on to the new tablet. Press it down firmly and it won't come unstuck. Or you can collect the pieces and tie them all up in a bag to be used for washing-up.

NEVER rub your soap on to a flannel. Instead, first wet the face with hot water. Then, rub your wet finger-tips over the soap tablet and gently massage your whole face. Rinse with cold water.

LUX TOILET SOAP
THE BEAUTY SOAP OF THE FILM STARS
3-OZ. TABLET (3½D.) FOR ONE COUPON
Weight nett when manufactured   Price includes Purchase Tax
A LEVER PRODUCT
TL 1264·151

WAR ON WASTE
The Government encouraged thriftiness and self-reliance with such slogans as 'Make Do and Mend', 'Grow Your Own Food', 'Dig for Victory' and 'Wage War on Waste'.

·· every available piece of land must be cultivated

GROW YOUR OWN FOOD
supply your own cookhouse

Government recipes invited readers to try their hand at Carrot Croquettes and Carrot Fudge, Patriotic Puddings and All-Clear Sandwiches. So-called 'Woolton Pie' – a disagreeable concoction of potatoes, parsnips and herbs – became something of a wartime joke. The Ministry also managed to get Spam, dried eggs and dried milk in quantities from the United States, and for the eggs, especially, some people came almost to feel a real affection. A Tynesider recalled of his wartime boyhood: 'We never starved but we ate some bloody funny things. Best was American dried egg. You poured a thin trickle into the frying pan, then as it cooked it blew up like a balloon, till it was 2in thick, like a big yellow hump-backed whale.'

Pigs' brains and cows' udders were eaten. Customers could have a modest-priced meal without coupons, but they had to be careful. Sometimes, having finished a juicy steak, the restaurant-goer might see a notice saying: 'Horse is Provided Here.'

Bread was never rationed in Britain during the war years, and despite its unappetising greyness the long, coarse 'National Loaf' had its admirers. Children often had it cooked, mashed with parsnips, a little sugar and some essence of banana, to make what passed for 'mashed bananas'.

'Dig for Victory' was one of the great wartime slogans, first launched in a broadcast of October 1939 when the Agriculture Minister, Sir Reginald Dorman-Smith, called for every able-bodied man and woman to dig an allotment in their spare time. Lawns and flower-beds were turned into vegetable gardens; office workers cultivated plots in town parks. The aim was to make Britain as self-sufficient in food as possible. Chickens, rabbits and even pigs were reared in town gardens.

'ANYTHING UNDER THE COUNTER?'
Although cigarettes and alcohol were never officially rationed, they were often in short supply. Many shopkeepers made a point of allocating their own limited stocks of small necessities to their favourite

GETTING AROUND
With petrol rationed, town gas was used to power some cars. But the gas was costly and bulky: 202 cubic feet (5.7 cubic metres) for one gallon (4.5 litres) of petrol. Steering was a nightmare.

customers. Housewives often finished their shopping by asking the shopkeeper 'AUC?' meaning 'Anything Under the Counter?'

'Make Do and Mend' was, above all, the order of the day. There were huge salvage drives in which scrap materials from rags to waste paper were collected and carted away to be reprocessed. Bones were salvaged to make glue for aircraft. In the great drive for scrap metals, householders' aluminium pots were collected to make Spitfire fighter planes, and parks, gardens and town houses were stripped of their ornamental iron railings, sacrificed to make ships and tanks.

In much the same spirit, ordinary people adapted service materials from army blankets to parachute silk to meet their fashion needs. Clothing was rationed from June 1941 on a points system: in principle, it allowed people to buy one complete new outfit a year.

Meanwhile, new 'Utility' clothing was introduced. To save fabric, men's trousers were made without turn-ups while women's skirts were short and straight, with no trimmings.

The women's magazines were packed with handy tips on how, for example, old lace curtains might be cut up to make a 'dashing little bolero', and every type of ingenuity was applied in the name of style. A woman from Walsall in the Midlands remembers how shoe polish and the colouring matter used in the gravy for the Sunday joint became indispensable fashion accessories: 'Stockings were in short supply so girls coloured their legs with tan cream or gravy browning – very nice until it rained! A friend would draw a line down the back of your legs, with an eyebrow pencil, for the seam.'

Even the design of tables and chairs was influenced by wartime shortages. The wood used and the amount of decoration was limited by government specifications. 'Utility furniture' was the name given to the resulting articles, which were plain but serviceable enough.

MAKE DO AND MEND

SAVINGS DRIVE
Britons handed over their aluminium utensils to be made into aircraft. At home, people 'made do' by mending old clothes with needle and thread.

THE PARAPHERNALIA OF WARTIME BRITAIN

While familiar household goods became hard to find, a wealth of new wartime items changed the texture of daily life.

For THE SIX YEARS of World War II the lives of British people were encumbered by a wholly unfamiliar range of everyday objects: ration-books and identity cards; the many symbols of officialdom, such as the air-raid warden's helmet; and foods such as Spam and dried milk. As many of the staples of the British diet were rationed, some people began to feel a curious affection for the substitutes.

Shops sold luminous discs for people to wear during the blackout, and luminous paint to dab on the doorbell. The colour of pillar-boxes changed; they were coated with a special yellow paint that turned red when there was poisonous blister-gas in the air.

MODEL SPITFIRE Schoolboys made models to help in identifying British and foreign aircraft. They were given recognition tests, with silhouettes flashed onto screens from magic lanterns.

POWDERED FOOD Britons became accustomed to dried milk and dried eggs. From 1942, one packet per person of dried egg (equivalent to a dozen eggs) was distributed every two months. It made rubbery omelettes and puddings which 'looked like linoleum tiles'. Condensed milk was made available on a points rationing system.

PROTECTING THE HOME Government leaflets gave advice on home defence against air raids, and methods were illustrated on cigarette cards and elsewhere. Windows were taped or papered against bomb blast, doors made gas-proof with rugs and tape. Newspapers advertised ready-filled sandbags at one shilling each.

WILLS'S CIGARETTES

WINDOW PROTECTION AGAINST BLAST

MAKING A DOOR GAS-PROOF

DIMMING DEVICE From early in 1940, car headlamps were supposed to be fitted with regulation ARP masks which allowed only narrow, horizontal slits of light. Some towns permitted 'glimmer lighting' by which pinpricks of illumination were aimed downwards from street lamps at road junctions.

HOME OFFICE

THE PROTECTION OF YOUR HOME AGAINST AIR RAIDS

READ THIS BOOK THROUGH
THEN
KEEP IT CAREFULLY

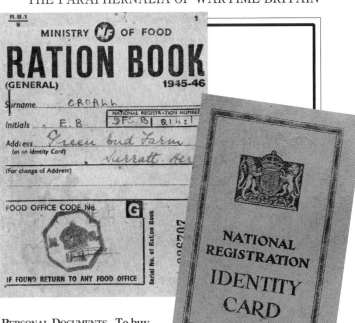

STIRRUP PUMP
The hand-operated pump was regarded as essential for putting out fires; buckets of water were kept in readiness. Attics were cleared out as precautions against incendiary bombs.

PERSONAL DOCUMENTS To buy restricted foods, people handed over their ration book to the shopkeeper, who removed the coupons (as well as taking the appropriate sum of money). The identity card, containing a personal number, had to be carried at all times and produced on demand.

in a raid—

Do not rush, take cover quietly, then others will do the same.

TIN HAT The helmet painted with a white 'W' helped to distinguish air-raid wardens among crowds of civilians. Wardens carried whistles to warn of raids and ensure that everyone was off the streets.

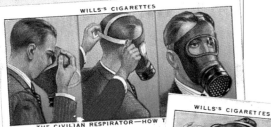

GAS MASKS 'Remember, chin in – right in – first, before you start to pull the straps over your head', ran the official instructions. The respirators looked alarming, and to calm the fears of small children the Government issued some brightly coloured examples, known as Mickey Mouses.

INSIGNIA The badge of the ARP service, which was mobilised as early as September 1938, during the Munich crisis.

NEWS AND ENTERTAINMENT

'We Never Closed,' was the proud boast of London's tiny Windmill Theatre –

a West End show place that stayed open through the worst of the Blitz. Music, dancing,

radio and film all helped to make wartime hardships easier for Britons to bear.

BOMBING RAIDS, petrol shortages and blacked-out streets all meant that ordinary people spent a lot of evenings at home. The radio served as a lifeline, and just about everyone crowded round their set to listen to the nine o'clock News on the BBC Home Service.

Standing on the cliffs of southern England during the Battle of Britain, for example, Charles Gardner gave vivid accounts of the dogfights overhead, with excited interjections: 'You've got him. Pump it into him. Pop-pop-pop – oh boy, oh boy, he's going down.'

It was over the radio that families heard Churchill's stirring broadcasts to the nation. On weekdays, at 8.15am, *Kitchen Front* broadcasts were made, giving information on food prices and availability.

Children's Hour did much to reassure the young with the soothing voice of 'Uncle Mac' (Derek McCulloch) and the humour of characters such as Larry the Lamb and Dennis the Dachshund. For adults, the great comedy hit was Tommy Handley's *ITMA* (*It's That Man Again*) – a true phenomenon of wartime broadcasting. The half-hour programme became such a feature of national life that, it was said, if Hitler chose to invade England between 8.30 and 9pm on a Thursday he would have an easy job of it,

because the whole country would be tuned in to Tommy Handley. A host of outlandish characters peopled the show. There was Mrs Mopp, the cleaner, with her catch-phrase, 'Can I do yer now, sir?', Funf, the bungling German spy, and the immortal Colonel Chinstrap who greeted every remark as if it were an offer of a drink with the words: 'I don't mind if I do.' Fast-moving, packed with wisecracks and dottily British, the show proved more of a morale booster than any government propaganda.

Propaganda there certainly was, however, and many more or less dull talks on the Home Service. For continual music and variety, millions tuned in to the Forces Programme which started broadcasting in February 1940 with 12 hours of light entertainment a day, from 11am to 11pm. Created for troops crowding canteens and billets, the programme also attracted a huge civilian audience and one of its great successes was *Sincerely Yours,* presented by Vera Lynn, the 'Forces' Sweetheart', billed as a 'sentimental half-hour

ON THE AIR The valve radio (left) was a key item in millions of British homes. Tommy Handley (above), star of the *ITMA* series, broadcasts with Dorothy Summers, the indomitable 'Mrs Mopp'.

REACHING EVERYONE
BBC reporters interview a
woman amid bombed-out ruins.
Above: *Lilli Marlene* was the
war's most popular melody.

linking the men in the forces with their womenfolk at home'. The singer's famous song of wartime separation, *We'll Meet Again,* was the signature tune.

The Brains Trust was another invention of the Forces Programme, and proved an astonishing success. The original idea was to settle servicemen's barrack-room arguments by putting questions before a panel. It had three regulars: the philosopher C.E.M. Joad, scientist Julian Huxley and retired naval man Commander A.B. Campbell. Questions ranged from the most abstruse scientific problems to such posers as 'Why can you tickle other people but you can't tickle yourself?'

AT YOUR LOCAL CINEMA

To escape the claustrophobic atmosphere of home, people went to the movies. They were prepared to queue for hours to get in every week and in wartime Britain some 25-30 million cinema tickets were sold each week. The big picture houses with their grandiose names – Majestic, Palace, Alhambra – created dream worlds where for a few pence the dark streets and the bombs could be forgotten.

The most popular movies were the adventure films, comedies, Westerns and musicals from the United States. Most successful of all was *Gone with the Wind* (1939), which played in London's West End non-stop from the spring of 1940 to the spring of 1944.

In contrast to Hollywood's offerings, many British films were dour and dutiful. *The Gentle Sex* (1943) was a case in point, documentary in treatment and dedicated to the part women were playing in embattled Britain. None the less, some outstanding British pictures came out of the war. One of them was *In Which We Serve* (1942), a superb patriotic piece starring and directed by Noël Coward and set around a torpedoed destroyer. Another was Laurence Olivier's *Henry V* (1944), filmed in Ireland. This inspiring, sometimes experimental production of Shakespeare's play made references to war which were as relevant to the 20th century as they were to the 15th.

In factory towns, cinemas sometimes screened messages to workers needed on the next shift. And during intervals, picture-goers were treated to recitals by the cinema organist. Requests were played, the most popular turning out to be *The White Cliffs of Dover,* Vera Lynn's hit song, which audiences seem never to have tired of hearing. In the home, people played songs on 78rpm records which scratchily reproduced the sound through steel needles and wind-

heard on children's lips as they pestered American servicemen. But these were never quite as affecting as the dreamier songs of longing and romance that captured the hopes of countless men and women. For many, the great song of the Blitz was *A Nightingale Sang in Berkeley Square*.

It was also the age of the big bands. The dance halls were the chief meeting places for men and women in wartime, where people of very different social classes came together as they never would have done before. With the great influx of Commonwealth and American troops, different nationalities mixed too. In earlier times, no respectable wife would have gone to a dance without her husband, but as the war dragged on, more and more went along for the fun and comradeship. The agony columns of women's magazines were full of letters from married women who had 'met a man at a dance' and drifted into infidelity.

A TONIC FOR THE TROOPS

At troop concerts, two stars from the industrial North of England were much in demand: ukelele-playing George Formby and Gracie Fields ('Our Gracie' to her fans). To help the war effort an organisation called ENSA was formed. The initials stood for Entertainments National Services Association, though

up gramophones. The war's biggest hit was the German *Lili Marleen*. It had been overheard by Eighth Army troops in North Africa and proved so popular that an English version, *Lilli Marlene – My Lilli of the Lamplight* was penned and recorded.

Topical songs promised an end to the blackout: *I'm Going to Get Lit Up (When the Lights Go On in London)* was an example. *Any Gum, Chum?* celebrated the GIs' presence in Britain with a catch-phrase often

BRITISH MADE
Classic British films which came out of the war included Noël Coward's *Brief Encounter* (1945). Celia Johnson and Trevor Howard starred as the suburban housewife and local doctor whose quiet love affair is set against the background of a dingy railway station.

CHEEK TO CHEEK London's 'Stage Door Canteen' was inspired by the original American club, which opened in Broadway, New York in March 1942.

wags preferred 'Every Night Something Awful' for this hastily organised army of professional artistes.

People also made their own entertainment.

Community singing accompanied by accordions helped to keep spirits up during the darkest days of the Blitz. *Yes, We Have No Bananas* and *Roll Out the Barrel* were two of the favourites of East Enders, while the nonsense song *Mairzy Doats and Dozy Doats* caught on like wildfire in 1944. In playgrounds, children adapted current melodies for their own purposes. Disney's *Snow White,* the first feature-length cartoon film, made in 1938, was hugely popular and the famous work song of the dwarfs became:

> *Whistle while you work*
> *Hitler is a twerp*
> *Goering's barmy*
> *So's his army*
> *Whistle while you work.*

People took increasingly to reading poetry and going to art exhibitions, however, and the biggest highbrow boom was in concert-going. The famous Henry Wood Promenade Concerts – or Proms – where a large part of the audience would traditionally stand or 'promenade' continued through periods of nightly bombing at the Queen's Hall in London. When that building was destroyed by fire they carried on at the Albert Hall. From October 1939 concert pianist Myra Hess was organising lunchtime recitals in the now empty National Gallery. The concerts continued throughout the war and were enormously popular – so much so that people lined up outside every day to get tickets.

LANCASHIRE LASS Gracie Fields entertains Scottish shipyard workers. She was much in demand despite temporary disapproval when she married her Italian producer, Monty Banks, just as Italy declared war.

33

PROPAGANDA MACHINES

All sides controlled the release of information to boost morale at home, and to demoralise the enemy.

UNDERGROUND PRESS Underground newspapers were published to keep up morale. Below: A German propaganda leaflet.

Je suis tombée, ô Churchill!
Où es-tu? Où sont tes soldats?

IT WAS SAID IN THE United States after Pearl Harbor that Japanese workmen near the naval base had cut huge arrows in the fields to guide Japanese aircraft towards their targets. Pure fantasy, of course – but the home front everywhere was a breeding ground for rumour.

With censorship in operation and everyone strained by anxiety, people's imaginations filled in the details whenever something strange or disastrous occurred. Many wild reports – like the one above – played on fears of the enemy's fiendish ingenuity. So, for example, Britons spoke in hushed voices of a German bomb so advanced that it could chase you round corners; and of a nun seen in a railway carriage who had apparently shown her ticket to the inspector with a big, hairy hand – she was really a Nazi paratrooper in disguise . . . or so the story went. Wild rumours circulated about foreign spies, bungling by the

JAIRMANY CALLING 'Lord Haw-Haw' made slanted remarks about coming air raids that some of his British audience found deeply unsettling.

government and an imminent invasion. Keeping public morale high was an obsession of the authorities in World War II, so that even a calamity like the withdrawal from Dunkirk was reported in Britain as if it were a triumph. A person could go on trial for spreading alarm or despondency. Addressing his anxious readers in Britain in May 1940, the comic poet A.P. Herbert wrote:

Do not believe the tale the milkman tells;
No troops have mutinied in Potters Bar.
Nor are there submarines in Tunbridge
*   Wells.*
The BBC will warn us when there are.

Edginess on the home front created an ideal climate for enemy propagandists to exploit, and the Nazis spread disquiet in Britain through the son of an Irish-born American, William Joyce. Nicknamed 'Lord Haw-Haw', Joyce was a former British Fascist who broadcast to Britain from Berlin. His sinister, hectoring voice announcing, 'Jairmany calling, Jairmany calling', became well known to 6 million listeners. Some found his show amusing, others tuned in in the hope of learning facts that the Ministry of Information was withholding.

Japan produced an equally notorious broadcaster in the shape of Iva Ikuko Toguri, nicknamed Tokyo Rose. Her 15-minute

radio show, broadcast to GIs in the Pacific, interspersed music with news and comment delivered in a flirtatious American accent (she was, in fact, an American-born Japanese). GIs in Italy were meanwhile tormented by the sexy voice of a lady known as Axis Sally. 'Hullo suckers', was how she began her Front Line Radio show, which mixed scratchy boogie-woogie tunes with tales of Allied setbacks and the names of POWs held in Rome. There were stories of draft-dodgers fooling around with GIs' girlfriends on the home front, and of hideous injuries sustained by American fighting men. 'Think it over', a show would end. 'Why

VOICE OF THE ENEMY Tokyo Rose's radio shows, transmitted across the Pacific region, were designed to demoralise the American GIs and naval crews who were serving in the region. After the war she was put on trial in the USA.

Kraft durch Freude!

"Ich habe jede Möglichkeit von vorn herein einkalkuliert." Hitler, 30.1.41

Hitler besichtigt das Modell, Berlin 1938

Der fertige Wagen in Libyen 1942

POPULATIONS abandonnées,

faites confian AU SOLDAT ALLEMA

FRIEND OR FOE? The Germans portrayed themselves as friendly occupiers and innocent victims. Below: Victory becomes a game.

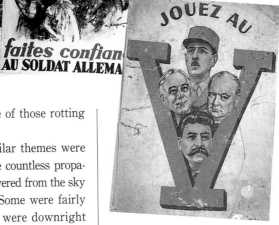

JOUEZ AU V

**DUNKIRK –
TWO VIEWS**

German and British newspapers gave very different accounts of Dunkirk:

'THE GREAT BATTLE OF ANNIHILATION
Altogether more than 1.2 million prisoners have fallen into German hands,

besides limitless amounts of war material . . . France's and Britain's finest troops are annihilated. England is now separated from France and exposed to a direct German attack. On June 4 this battle of annihilation came to an end with the fall of Dunkirk.'
Signal, German wartime picture magazine, 1940

'BLOODY MARVELLOUS
For days past thousands upon thousands of our brave men of the B.E.F. have been pouring through a port somewhere in England, battle-worn, but, thank God, safe and cheerful in spite of weariness. We may hope that already at least half of that gallant force has been withdrawn from the trap planned for them by Nazi ruthlessness . . . Praise in words is a poor thing for this huge and heroic effort. But praise we must offer for all engaged, and for the brilliant leadership in the field . . . Praise, then, for him and for them! "A bloody marvellous show", says a high officer.'
Daily Mirror, Saturday, June 1, 1940.

should you be one of those rotting carcasses?'

These and similar themes were worked over in the countless propaganda leaflets showered from the sky by Axis aircraft. Some were fairly gruesome; others were downright obscene. The more attractive served as pin-ups, but for multitudes in the ration-hit nations, propaganda leaflets served above all as a handy source of toilet paper.

The Axis powers were by no means alone in exploiting these methods. Allied agencies set up their own 'black radio' stations to spread despondency in enemy territory, and a British body which became known as the Political Warfare Executive (PWE) was responsible for inventing 'sibs', plausible stories that were likely to damage enemy morale. Designed for export, they were first tried out in London clubs and canteens before being passed on to Occupied Europe. Hitler was mad – his generals had seen him chewing the carpet in one of his rages. Invading Britain was pointless – the Allies had invented a means of setting the sea ablaze. Furthermore, a colossal tonnage of propaganda leaflets was distributed across the Axis countries by Allied bombers.

ON THE AIR American boys take part in a two-way radio exchange with their counterparts in London, talking about the effect the war was having on their lives.

FOREIGN FRIENDS AND FOES

Wartime Britain was surprisingly cosmopolitan: French sailors, bush-hatted Australian soldiers and

exuberant GIs were familiar figures on the streets. There were German soldiers occupying the

Channel Islands, and, of course, the spectre of enemy spies everywhere.

I N JANUARY 1942 the first US servicemen began to arrive in the British Isles to set up military bases. About 1.5 million were to pass through the United Kingdom before the war was over – friendly, outgoing types in stylishly tailored uniforms who spread like a tide across the countryside from East Anglian air bases to West Country army camps. The GIs (so-called because their equipment was all labelled Government Issue) were better paid than their British counterparts and wherever they went they were prone to lavish local people with the fruits of their PX (post-exchange) or camp stores.

From the PX came cartons of Lucky Strike and Camel cigarettes; precious nylon stockings that took the place of the silk stockings that had long vanished from the shops; scented soap; razor blades of pre-war quality; chocolate; ice cream and more. Gum-chewing, jeep-driving and open-handed with gifts, the 'Yanks' seemed impossibly glamorous – at least to school-children and their older sisters. And their camps and bases were like little pockets of America from which a wealth of things new to British life would spill.

American slang swept the nation. Children also learned of comic-book heroes such as Superman, with his X-ray vision, and supercop Dick Tracy with his two-way wrist TV. English schoolboys who had thrilled to the heroics of Arsenal or Tottenham footballers now slouched in corners, clicking their

GOOD TIMES American soldiers drink coffee at the Rainbow Corner, a wartime club for GIs near Piccadilly Circus in London. Right: a GI offers British boys candy – a major attraction with sweet rationing in force in Britain.

fingers to the rhythms of swing and jazz gods such as Benny Goodman, Artie Shaw and Fats Waller. The American aircraft, with exciting names like Grumann Hellcat, were much admired. A Tyneside man who was aged 13 at the time of the American invasion remembers gawping at the statistics of the Flying Fortress, with its bomb-sight so accurate, so it was claimed, that it could drop a bomb into a pickle-barrel from 20,000 feet, 'and the American troop carriers, huge four-engined monoplanes that made our old biplanes look like rubbish from the Science Museum'.

If the schoolboys were impressed, their sisters were overwhelmed. It was through the GIs that many British girls received their first lessons in jitterbugging, a dance craze that spread with such enthusiasm that many ballrooms had to ban it to protect their sprung floors. The jitterbug was for the uninhibited – like the GIs themselves. The American visitors took British girls to the best local clubs and restaurants, caring nothing for distinctions of rank and class prevalent in British society.

The Yanks were sufficiently well paid to 'live it up' in a style unknown to local women, many of whom were doing 12-hour shifts in munitions factories and the like. British girls were captivated. Some 80,000 were to become GI brides, emigrating to America.

Obviously, British men felt less delirious enthusiasm for the GIs, who were often thought of as 'overpaid, oversexed and over here'. The American authorities were aware of the tensions that their relative affluence might create, and the official booklet of advice to US forces reminded servicemen: 'Stop and think before you sound off about lukewarm beer or cold boiled potatoes, or the way English cigarettes taste. If British civilians look dowdy and badly dressed, it is not because they do not like good clothes or know how to wear them. All clothing is rationed.'

Overall, the American arrival was welcomed by a nation very much aware of the crucial part they were playing in the Allied struggle.

SPIES AND ALIENS

In 1940, it was whispered that invading Germans were being parachuted into Britain dressed as nuns – an example of the rumours that circulated in Britain during the war. The edgy atmosphere was not

OVER HERE American service personnel were issued with a guide to help them come to terms with the British way of life. It contained much sensible and practical advice. 'The British have movies (which they call "cinemas") but the great place of recreation is the "pub". Don't show off or brag or bluster – "swank" as the British say. Don't make fun of British speech or accents. NEVER criticize the King or Queen.'

NIGHT CLUB Segregated from white American servicemen, black GIs mixed freely with British women.

I Spy A poster by 'Fougasse' warns against spies. The few real German agents in Britain were of low calibre. (Picked up after landing by parachute near St Albans, Karel Richter was unable to explain why he was wearing three sets of underclothes.)

reach enemy ears through stray conversations. But the campaign had the effect of suggesting that the Germans possessed vast spy networks in Britain, a notion wildly out of scale with reality.

The people who suffered most through spy mania were the many thousands of civilians living in Britain who had been born in what were now enemy states. In 1939, for example, there were 68,000 German, Austrian and Czech nationals in Britain – many of them refugees from Nazi persecution. Most had been rounded up by the summer of 1940, and were being held in bleak transit camps pending internment. In June, when Italy entered the war, there were attacks on Italian restaurants and ice-cream parlours. Partly for their own safety, 4000 Italians were interned too.

THE OCCUPATION OF THE CHANNEL ISLANDS

They crowded British streets – German soldiers in field-grey uniform, buying rounds in local pubs, winking at shop-girls in Boots the Chemist, marching, too, along the country lanes singing German songs. The occupation of the Channel Islands is one of the war's oddest episodes. Jersey, Guernsey and the

diminished by government posters reminding people that 'Careless Talk Costs Lives!', and 'Walls Have Ears!', and exhorting them to 'Keep It Under Your Hat!' or 'Be Like Dad – Keep Mum'.

The official worry was that information about the positions of armed forces, munitions and ships might

ROUND UP Women held in Britain as aliens are sent to the Isle of Man for internment. 'Everyone thought it would be like a concentration camp', one recalled. But by the summer of 1943 most had been released.

JERSEY, 1940 Residents mingle with German soldiers gathered in the Royal Parade, St Helier, to hear a German military band. The *Evening Post* (right) conveys the German Commandant's orders, including hours of curfew and a ban on private cars.

smaller islands of Alderney and Sark all succumbed without a struggle to Hitler's invasion forces in the summer of 1940. People were overwhelmed by the strangeness of their situation, for no part of Britain had been occupied by another foreign power since 1066. Suddenly, the swastika was flying over familiar public buildings. At the local Gaumont cinema on Guernsey posters advertised Nazi propaganda films like the feature-length documentary *Sieg Im Westen* (*Victory in the West*).

The islanders were treated leniently by comparison with many other peoples of Occupied Europe – at least at the outset. Rationing and curfews were imposed, of course, and there was censorship of the Press and books. But German soldiers played football with local men, and children sometimes picked up their marching songs. The occupying troops went to local dances, too, and often turned the heads of impressionable girls. Women who went out with German soldiers were dubbed 'Jerrybags' by other islanders, but there were large numbers of them, attracted by the soldiers' good looks and generosity. Privations were certainly known, however. Root vegetables became the staple of the islanders' diet and families learned to make tea from blackberry or rose leaves. The soap shortage was so bad that even the smallest cut was prone to fester and one doctor gave the name 'Occupation ulcer' to a type of leg sore.

From 1942, the Germans made the islands a key part of their Atlantic Wall defences against Allied invasion. Colossal resources of steel and concrete were poured in to build blockhouses and anti-tank walls, while thousands of foreign slave labourers were imported to work under the auspices of the Organisation Todt, which was responsible, among other things, for military construction. Several islanders took risks to try and help the handful of escapers. But there could be no assistance for the inmates of Alderney. The isle's population had been almost entirely evacuated, and it became a site for SS camps patrolled by guards with dogs overseeing haggard, pyjama-uniformed prisoners.

SPY KIT

The Allies' special agencies lavished fantastic ingenuity on equipment for clandestine work behind enemy lines.

IT WAS NO SURPRISE to see a man or woman lugging a battered leather suitcase through the streets of Hitler's Europe. The occupied lands teemed with people on the move: conscripted workers, refugees, evacuees and many other innocent travellers. But among the dishevelled crowds were a few individuals with secrets to hide: foreign agents, for example, and escaped POWs hoping to pass unnoticed among all the shabbily dressed citizens. That ill-fitting coat might have been tailored from a blanket in a prisoner-of-war camp. That leather suitcase might conceal a Mark II radio transmitter.

The British SOE's operatives were trained at spy schools situated in various country houses scattered around Beaulieu, in the New Forest area of southern England. Here they learned how to pick a lock; memorise a cover story; set up a rendezvous; lose a 'tail'; write in code; and kill in silence. The agency also had its own tailors who made clothing styled for continental Europe, with foreign labels stitched into the linings. Before departure, agents were issued with lethal cyanide capsules, known as 'L pills', for optional use if there was a risk of torture.

SPY DROP A British Westland 'Lysander I' aeroplane. This type of plane was adapted for landing special agents in occupied France and picking them up again at the end of their missions. They also helped to rescue escaped POWs.

DEADLY QUIET The Welrod silent pistol, a one-shot, 7.65 mm weapon whose 12-inch silencer could be detached from the butt and hidden in a trouser-leg.

PASSPORT British servicemen were issued with documents that they could hand over if caught by the enemy.

EVASION EQUIPMENT Airmen were issued with silk maps that would not alert enemy ears by rustling. **Right:** compasses were concealed in objects like cigarette lighters and buttons.

Я англичанин

"Ya Anglicháhnin" (Pronounced as spelt)

Пожалуйста сообщите сведения обо мне в Британскую Военную Миссию в Москве

Please communicate my particulars to British Military Mission Moscow

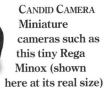

KEEPING IN CONTACT Cipher machines were used to produce messages in code, and microdot messages were smuggled across Europe.
Right: From cupboards and attics, radio operators nicknamed 'pianists' received and transmitted messages in Morse code on radios that fitted into suitcases.

CANDID CAMERA Miniature cameras such as this tiny Rega Minox (shown here at its real size) could be concealed in the palm of the hand. They were developed for clandestine photography behind enemy lines.

FORGED IDENTITY False identity documents were essential for agents, stranded airmen and POWs on the run. Allied air crews carried passport photographs in case they needed forged papers.

BRITAIN AT WORK

Britain's war effort brought together people from very different sections of society and

introduced a whole new range of jobs: society girls driving trains and tractors; young 'Bevin Boys'

working down the mines; and Italian and German prisoners of war working in the fields.

IN MARCH 1941 Ernest Bevin, Minister of Labour, announced the call-up of British women to help in the war effort. Registration of 20 and 21-year-olds was announced for the following month, and though pregnant women and mothers with young children were exempt, it was already clear that life at one social level would be radically affected. Among better-off families, one consequence was a sudden drop in the number of girls available for domestic service. The advertising columns of daily papers were crammed with appeals for cooks and housemaids.

One vital need was for women to work in munitions factories, filling shells with explosives as many had done voluntarily in World War I. But there was a wealth of other options and, as more and more women were conscripted, they found work in tank and aircraft factories, civil defence, nursing, transport and other key occupations, so releasing men for the armed forces.

Women could choose to join one of the auxiliary services – the Women's Royal Naval Service (WRNS), the Women's Auxiliary Air Force (WAAF) or the Auxiliary Territorial Service (ATS). Still another option was to become a member of the Women's Land Army, which had been formed in World War I to provide help on farms and which was revived in July 1939. Women manned anti-aircraft batteries, drove trains and tractors, operated cranes and became proficient spot-welders. In fact, they did just about everything except go down the mines.

DOING YOUR BIT

By 1943 it was almost impossible for a woman under 40 to avoid 'doing her bit': about 90 per cent of single women and 80 per cent of married women were engaged in one or another kind of war work. Many women enjoyed their transformed lives, with the chance to earn wages, and the new challenges and

---

EYEWITNESS

SCHOOLDAYS IN ST ALBANS

❝ At the grammar school I went to in St Albans we adopted a mine-sweeper, and the older girls knitted balaclavas and gloves and wrote to the sailors. The replies that came were read out on Friday mornings in assembly. I remember one rather embarrassed captain or naval officer appeared, very red-faced and tongue-tied among hundreds of girls. He tried to thank us very much, but we all just stared at this officer ... We always had to sing *For Those in* *Peril on the Sea*; I always remember feeling very affected by it, especially at the time the convoys were being continually decimated. I can remember one of my schoolfriends standing in the playground rather quiet, and the other children said: "Oh well, his father was on the *Hood*." We never gave much sympathy, we just accepted it, that was it, your father's dead. ❞

From the recollections of Jean Stafford, a schoolgirl at the time.

1940 Jean Stafford with her mother

WORKING GIRLS Women toil alongside men to make and test barrage balloons at the Dunlop rubber factory in Manchester. Inset: 'Land Girls', members of the Women's Land Army, doing the farmwork.

new freedoms. But they did not get equal pay with men, nor did they get real opportunities for promotion. The foul language and blue jokes that were routine in factories shocked many sensitive spirits, and the hours were gruelling.

Fancy clothing was out. The working woman often wore trousers or dungarees instead of a skirt and, with 'Cover Your Hair for Safety' a slogan of the time, tied a scarf around her head. It was often done up in a headsquare turban – a distinctive wartime style which helped to create an almost uniform look. Music blared continually in factories. The BBC's *Music While You Work* provided the daily ration of tunes – at the height of the war over 8000 factories covering more than 4 million workers received the programme, and one manager reported that when the radio was shut down for a week there was a 20 per cent drop in output. A woman ship-builder recalled that the programme was all the rage in her works, though it had to compete constantly with the noises of cranes and the pounding of heavy hammers on steel plates. 'So we had it in the canteen, deafeningly, so that you couldn't hear what anyone said. The only time there was anything like a hush was when everyone was swooning over Bing Crosby.'

Accommodation had to be found for the vast membership of the Women's Land Army, which included waitresses, hairdressers and typists all hoping to be turned into farm hands. At its maximum strength in 1943, the Land Army numbered more than 80,000 women, all needing billets and uniforms. The

WORRIED BLUE EYES

FROM *WOMAN* MAGAZINE, 1942

I am serving in the Forces and find I am going to have a baby. Two men could be responsible, but I don't know which. Both have offered to marry me, but I can't decide which. Would it be better to throw them both over and make a fresh start?

Much better. You don't love either of them and whoever marries you will never feel sure of you. Get over this trouble, make up your mind to be morally stronger in the future, and marry when you find a man you can really love; moreover a man who will respect you before marriage.

WOMEN AT WAR Magazines for women reflected the social changes brought by the war.

Land Girls were kitted up in green jerseys, brown breeches, brown felt slouch-hats and cotton blouses. Land Girls were trained in batches of 30 or more and conditions of service were arduous. A working week of 50 hours was compulsory. They were allowed one week's paid holiday a year. Milking, ploughing, weeding, hoeing, muck-spreading and harvesting were among the chores, along with more specialised jobs such as rat-catching. In winter there were ditches to clear and hedges to trim. It was all back-breaking work, often carried out in appalling weather conditions, and many a recruit who had been enticed by cheery posters of Land Girls cradling lambs found herself bitterly disillusioned. None the less, figures showed that the Land Girls made an important contribution to wartime farming.

Besides the novel sight of women on tractors, country people also got used to seeing gangs of Italian and (later) German prisoners of war working in the fields. Italian prisoners from the Mediterranean theatre of war were being used from the summer of 1941. They were at first confined to camps and hostels, and were guarded by soldiers as they worked, but restrictions were later relaxed so that some lived and worked – unguarded – on farms. In accordance with the Geneva Convention the POWs were paid a small daily wage, and despite some early hostility they came to be regarded almost with affection.

From 1944 German POWs were also working in the fields, winning a reputation as harder workers than their Axis allies (they were never put to work side by

WOMEN WILL WORK IF CHI... ARE C

OUR CHILDR SAFE E WIL OR

WE WANT WAR WORK WE WANT NURSERIES

NURSERIES FOR KIDS!... WAR WORK FOR MOTHERS!

CHILDREN'S CRUSADE In response to a Government appeal, some British schoolboys volunteered for the coalmines. These are starting training at Markham Main Colliery, near Doncaster, September 1943. Right: mothers keen to do war work protest at the shortage of nurseries in London.

side with Italians for fear of trouble). Few escape attempts were made by either nation's prisoners, and no Axis POW ever managed to flee home direct from the British Isles. The German flying ace Franz von Werra, famed as 'The One Who Got Away', made the only successful bid for freedom in January 1941 by jumping a train in Canada and crossing into the then neutral United States.

Other novelties of the wartime working scene were the so-called Bevin Boys. By 1941, Ernest Bevin had won the right to tell just about any adult aged 14 to 65 what job they had to do, and in December 1943 he took a very unusual measure. Following a sharp drop in coal production, he sent a proportion of young men called up for National Service to work in the mines instead of the armed forces. One in ten were to work in the coal industry, by a ballot of their registration numbers. The recruits, known as Bevin Boys, counted themselves unlucky. Only 15,000 of them actually served at the coal face, however, and like so many other wartime experiences, it brought together people from very different sections of society who would never have met under other circumstances.

LENDING A HAND German prisoners of war sort potatoes. There were 500,000 German POWs in Britain towards the end of the war, and they were used chiefly to make up the shortage of farm labourers. The Geneva Convention forbade dangerous or military work.

WEDDINGS IN WARTIME

In wartime especially, love is precious. Weddings in

the fighting nations were a symbol of hope for the future.

I N BRITAIN and the United States, marriage boomed during the early war years as couples rushed to seal the banns before overseas service brought separation.

In 1940 the marriage rate in England and Wales rose to 11.2 per thousand (the pre-war rate was between 8 and 9). Thousands of Americans went to the altar after Pearl Harbor, and the marriage bonanza was especially large in areas like Seattle and San Diego, with their military bases.

In Occupied France, however, the marriage rate dropped to record lows. Declining marriage rates were also registered in Italy and in Germany – despite Nazi exhortations to bear children for the Reich.

UNDERGROUND UNION **A bomb shelter in Paris is the setting for this photograph taken in 1944.**

HOLY WEDLOCK **A British fusilier and his bride pick their way through the debris of a Catholic church in Blitz-torn London, 1940.**

THE WEDDING PHOTOGRAPH

6 We walked to the vestry and out into the rectory garden. Then, while the planes were battling for a life and death struggle overhead, we stood quietly for our photographs to be taken. Suddenly, without warning, a German plane flew in low over the house and released a bomb – I shouted to the photographer who was under a black velvet cloth trying to take the photo, "Look out, he's dropping bombs!" The man just shouted back from under the cloth, "Never mind about the bomb, JUST SMILE". 9

Joan Wildish, wartime bride.

WESTWARD HO GI brides sail in the *Queen Mary* to begin new lives in America, February 1946.

TO HAVE AND TO HOLD More than 80,000 GIs, like the corporal above, took British brides home to the United States. Right: the poignancy of wartime romance is captured as Ronald Reagan weds Joan Leslie in *This is the Army* (1943).

NAZI MARRIAGES The mass SS and SA wedding (right) was a non-religious ceremony. The document above is part of an *Ahnenpass* which every German couple had to obtain. It gave details of their forebears as evidence of 'racial purity'.

STARTING OUT A London bride examines her furniture permit. This was needed by any newly-weds wanting to buy new furniture.

PEDAL POWER A honeymoon couple in Rome begin married life with a bike ride. Petrol rationing and laws restricting the use of private cars meant that few could enjoy the luxury of a motorised send-off.

THE EMPIRE AND DOMINIONS

Japanese bombs fell on Darwin, Australia and there were air raids on Calcutta. Barbed wire lined

beaches in South Africa while Canadians gave up their aluminium pots for salvage. World War II

was a truly global conflict – and Britain's colonies and Dominions were fully involved.

BOTH AUSTRALIA and New Zealand quickly followed Britain into the war, and after Pearl Harbor the two Dominions were to serve as important bases for American troops. Fear of invasion was widespread as the Japanese came relentlessly closer through the islands to the north.

Australia felt herself a nation under siege. Blackout was enforced, coastlines were fortified and cities protected by searchlights and ack-ack batteries. From 1942, moreover, Australian families were to know the terror of bombing raids. Darwin in the north suffered the worst – much of the city centre was wiped out in an air raid that began before 10am on February 19, 1942. Panic spread as the bombs rained down on its crowded harbour area, killing some 300 people and wounding 400 more. Looting followed, and there was a mass exodus of militia and civilians streaming south. In all, more than 100 Japanese bombing raids were mounted on the north coast, though the Government censored news and the general public heard about very few of the raids. The Darwin attack could not, of course, be entirely hushed up, but the damage was minimised and the casualties were officially numbered at only 17.

As a precautionary measure, 6780 Australians were interned during the war – more than half of them of Italian origin. Rationing was introduced for clothing and some foods – tea, sugar and coffee – and as in Britain, suburban families took to digging up their lawns to grow vegetables. Petrol was heavily rationed too, and many motorists were reduced to using large and cumbersome charcoal burners, called gas producers, attached to their cars. John Dedman, Minister for War Organisation of Industry, won notoriety through banning the manufacture of inessentials that ranged from lawnmowers to patterned

RALLYING ROUND Australia helped the Allied cause by sending much-needed food supplies as well as contributing 680,000 servicemen like those on the right.

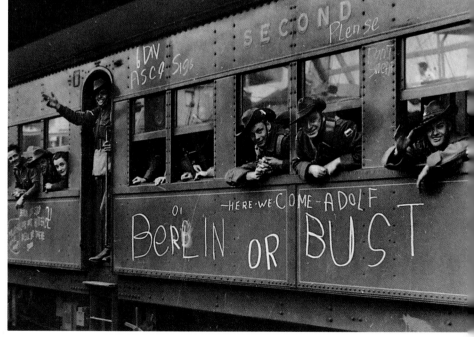

socks. Australian men took up the single-breasted two-piece Victory suit, without trouser turn-ups; their wives cooked them Austerity loaves and Austerity beef.

Many women also joined the Women's Land Army, or took over men's jobs to free them for active service. Even the normally shunned Aboriginal people achieved some slight progress towards integration with the white population through service in the armed forces and employment in the construction industry.

American aid and influence grew to such an extent that by the end of the war more than 60 per cent of Australian imports previously supplied from Britain were coming from the United States. Coca-Cola was first bottled in Australia during the war, and Reader's Digest started printing an Australian edition.

THE FRENCH CONNECTION

Unlike Australia and New Zealand, Canada was a Dominion with a large and influential non-British section of the population. Many French-speakers in Quebec were reluctant to support what was seen after

---

SOUTH AFRICANS AT WAR
Barbed wire entangles the beaches of Durban and a giant map outside the City Hall keeps people informed of the war's progress. No civilian deaths were recorded, but families grieved for the 9000 South Africans killed in action. In Britain, posters like the one shown right reminded people of South Africa's material contribution.

THE EMPIRE'S STRENGTH

DO YOU KNOW THAT SOUTH AFRICA

is not only by far the largest producer of gold, but also a great agricultural country, exporting wool, fruit, sugar, and dairy products: that chrome and manganese for armaments are also valuable exports.

THESE ARE THE SINEWS OF WAR

the fall of France in 1940 as an essentially British fight, and were as likely to align themselves with the collaborationist Vichy Government as with de Gaulle's Free French movement.

It took a three-day debate in Parliament before the Government declared war, and conscription for overseas service was approved only in 1942 after a plebiscite. Rationing was introduced but it was light by British standards, liquor and car tyres being the items in shortest supply. Unemployment, however, vanished almost overnight as a million people found work in the war industry.

Life on Canada's home front had much in common with the American experience. In the drive for economies, people were exhorted to 'Use it Up, Wear it Out, Make it Do and Do Without'. There were no mass bombings; it was above all as a gigantic provider that Canada found a role, turning out manpower, ships,

---

PAPER SAVING

To aid wartime economies the New Zealand Government told its citizens to use both sides of every sheet of paper. Unfortunately, the message was put across via large, paper-consuming posters. To save paper in South Africa, postage stamps were issued in half their normal size.

LOYAL DOMINION A Canadian poster of 1942 invites people to buy victory bonds – similar to the United States' war bonds – while (right) a Canadian couple entertain RAF trainees in their home. Canada was an important base for airmen on training courses run by the Empire Air Training Scheme.

vehicles, aircraft, weapons, munitions and food for the war effort. Halifax, the closest North American harbour to Britain, was a great gathering place for Atlantic convoys, bustling with continuous activity.

There was plenty of activity, too, at Durban and other big South African ports that were staging posts for Allied servicemen heading for Egypt and the Far East. Thousands of Italian prisoners of war taken in North Africa were shipped back to South Africa and large numbers of them were to settle there after the war. Privations, especially shortages of petrol, were experienced here as elsewhere.

Segregation, inevitably, lent a unique character to the South African experience of the home front. About 125,000 blacks joined the forces, though they were only permitted to serve as drivers, labourers and servants, and were forbidden to carry arms. With mines and factories working at full stretch, more and more blacks were needed in industry and the Government was forced to relax its colour bar to some extent.

India supplied more than 2 million of her people for the Allied armed forces – the largest voluntary recruitment in world history. And their efforts were all the more remarkable because the country had been

declared at war by the British Viceroy without consulting the Indian people. As a result, the existing struggle for independence intensified. Some Europeans were beaten up by crowds shouting 'Quit India', and guards were posted along railway lines to protect trains from sabotage. There were air raids on Calcutta, and the overall effect of Japanese success was to shake confidence in the Raj.

A further dimension to the drama in India was added by the outbreak of an appalling famine in Bengal in 1943. Hordes of starving Bengalis wandered the country to die by the roadside or in the streets of the cities. One and a half million people died as a result of the famine and ensuing epidemics.

Despite these colossal upheavals the war gave a tremendous boost to Indian industry and the country served as an immense supply centre for Allied forces. European women in India learned ARP drill, worked in offices and helped out in hospitals – not just as nurses, for it was during the war that the Indian Medical Service recruited women doctors for the first time. Some joined the armed forces to serve as drivers or cipher clerks. Others ran canteens or put on concerts to entertain the troops.

USA: THE ARSENAL OF DEMOCRACY

As can be seen from the wreckage-strewn Naval Air Station at

Pearl Harbor, Japan's assault force of torpedo planes and bombers caused

massive damage. More than 2400 lives were lost too. But the surprise attack

on the morning of December 7, 1941, also brought the full armed and industrial

might of the United States into the battle for democracy. From Hollywood to New York,

American life was galvanised by the struggle.

AMERICA GOES TO WAR

All through the 1930s, the United States had struggled to free itself from the Depression.

Despite the suffering and hardship of war, the country welcomed the boost that defence

spending gave to the economy.

IN 1939, when war broke out in Europe, most Americans favoured neutrality for their country. The United States was unprepared for war at this time, possessing only a small and ill-equipped volunteer army. By the summer of 1940, however, Americans were facing the disquieting fact that Hitler was master of Europe. President Roosevelt, determined to help embattled Britain and her allies, pressed for congressional action. In September the Selective Service Act was passed, introducing the first peacetime draft in American history. The Lend Lease programme was also approved to make aid to Britain easier. And on December 30, 1940, families tuning in to their radios heard the President declare that the United States must become the arsenal of democracy.

Japan's surprise attack on the US base at Pearl Harbor destroyed the last vestiges of isolationist feeling, and American industry now turned to full-scale war production. From 1941 to 1945 the USA was to build over 250,000 aircraft, almost 90,000 tanks, 350 destroyers and 200 submarines. Assembly lines were moving round the clock to make weaponry; by 1944 the United States was producing more than 40 per cent of the world's arms.

The achievements of industrialist Henry J. Kaiser in particular are remembered. For it was he who pioneered the revolutionary techniques of prefabrication and assembly that sent 597 identical liberty ships rolling down the slipways. In order to keep the flow of supplies across the Atlantic going, these freighters had to be built faster than German U-boats could sink them. Using standardised designs and ready-made sections, Kaiser was able to cut the average work time on a liberty ship from 200 days to 42 days.

There were more innovations besides. At a plant in Connecticut, Igor Sikorsky opened the world's first helicopter assembly line. And colossal federal funds were poured into the development of an atomic bomb at secret plants in Oak Ridge, Tennessee, and Los Alamos, New Mexico. This immense awakening of American industry ended the Great Depression of the 1930s. Unemployed men in their millions were drawn into the national effort, and the working week was increased from 40 to 48 hours.

With the armed forces siphoning off multitudes for combat, 6 million American women were added to the labour force. The Government encouraged the trend with posters urging women to 'Do the job HE left behind'. The archetypal working woman, wearing overalls and bandanna, was celebrated in the propaganda figure of 'Rosie the Riveter', a new national heroine portrayed in cartoons and in song for doing her patriotic bit in war production. There was even a movie, *Rosie the Riveter* (1944), which starred the glamorous B-movie star Jane Frazee.

By the standards of other countries involved in the

> ## DID YOU KNOW?
>
> In 1942, when Civil Defense preparations were at their height, America's best-selling book was the official Red Cross handbook on first aid. It sold more than 8 million copies – though it never appeared in the best-seller lists, being classified as a pamphlet.

HEADLINE NEWS Reports of the Pearl Harbor attack shook America. 'I knew that this was a turning point,' recalled a Chicago man, 'that our lives would never be the same again.'

The New York Times.

LATE CITY EDITION

"All the News That's Fit to Print"

VOL. XCI No. 30,684. NEW YORK, MONDAY, DECEMBER 8, 1941. THREE CENTS

JAPAN WARS ON U.S. AND BRITAIN; MAKES SUDDEN ATTACK ON HAWAII; HEAVY FIGHTING AT SEA REPORTED

CONGRESS DECIDED | TOKYO ACTS FIRST | SOVIET UNION | CANADA | GUAM BOMBED; ARMY SHIP IS SUNK

U. S. Fliers Head North From Manila—

FOUR FREEDOMS This classic poster from wartime America shows four paintings by the artist Norman Rockwell, all celebrating democratic and patriotic values as experienced in small-town American life.

fighting, American women were already well on their way to establishing the principle of female equality. The 200,000 who joined the armed services in World War II received equal pay. The money was good enough to trigger a huge migration of country and small-town girls towards defence plants and large urban centres, their numbers swollen by the movement of wives and girlfriends keen to stay close to their men at military camps.

Writer James Jones has recalled the atmosphere of 'wild gaiety and rollicking despair' that characterised the towns and cities near the camps and war

THE ALL-AMERICAN WAR

Have a coke', 'The Pause that Refreshes' … Catch phrases such as these kept the name of America's number-one soft drink before the public throughout World War II. Despite the impact of sugar rationing, Coca-Cola managed to make itself one of the most widely distributed products of wartime.

The success of the five-cent drink was chiefly the work of top executive Robert J. Woodruff, who persuaded the army and navy, early in the war, that his refreshing non-alcoholic beverage perfectly

Chocolate is a Fighting Food!

So supplies of chocolate products for those at home are limited.

If you can't always get your favorite Nestle's Chocolate Bar, Semi-Sweet Morsels or Ever-Ready Cocoa, remember your dealer's supply is restricted. The needs of our armed forces come first.

CHOCOLATE GOES TO WAR Tons of cocoa were consumed daily by the American armed forces, leaving little for civilians on the home front. Advertisements like this kept brand names in view even when supplies were unavailable.

matched the needs of America's fighting men.

Coca-Cola followed the flag, travelling with the troops all over the world. And so did the manufacturing plants, which were set up as far afield as Australia. By 1945 the firm's advertisements could boast: 'Our fighting men meet up with Coca-Cola many places overseas, where it's bottled on the spot.' The operation was costly, but the whole world got a taste for the drink that added 'life and sparkle to living', and in the decade after the war Coca-Cola would experience an

INTERNATIONAL EVENT By 1945, when this advertisement appeared, Coca-Cola had been introduced to servicemen of many nations.

astonishing global expansion.

Philip K. Wrigley achieved similar results for his chewing-gum firm. So skilfully did he persuade the authorities that chewing gum was an essential 'war material' that, at the request of the army, he supplied a stick of gum for every pack of 'K' or combat rations. His firm even took over the rations packing.

The gum, it was said, helped to relieve the GIs' thirst; it also relieved tension at times when tobacco smoking was banned; and even helped to keep their teeth clean. Wrigley also supplied gum to war workers in arms factories, convincing bosses that chewing gum meant fewer trips to the water fountain or the smoking area.

From Well Before Pearl Harbor
Right Up to the Present Time

America's Gallant Armed Forces Have
Received a Steady Supply of Arms for Victory

MASS-PRODUCED BY CHEVROLET

ARMS FOR VICTORY Chevrolet was among the big manufacturers supplying the armed forces. Left: One of the 597 identical Liberty ships rolls down the slipway at a Baltimore shipyard.

factories. His own hang-out was a once-chic hotel called the Peabody in downtown Memphis: 'The great influx of servicemen had taken it over from the local gentry, and at just about any time of the day or night there were always between half a dozen and a dozen wide-open drinking parties going on in the rooms and suites.'

The moral laxity that resulted prompted the authorities at some war factories to hire 'Dorothy Dixes' – matronly figures whose job was to minimise work-time liaisons and to serve as counsellors for girls who were facing personal problems. Some commentators feared for the survival of the American

family unit, as people spoke increasingly of the 'latchkey kids' left to fend for themselves while 'Mom' was off on the assembly line.

Yet families did survive, and despite the exhaustion of working a 48-hour week there were some new comforts. War factories introduced piped music, for example, and coffee breaks. A salesgirl at a department store found that she could double or even treble her pay by switching to an aircraft plant. By 1944 the signs of booming prosperity were all about, and sales of luxury goods such as fur coats and jewellery were flourishing. Restaurants were packed – though customers had to wait interminably for their meals because there were too few employees serving at the tables.

ADVANCES ON THE HOME FRONT

American blacks had at first been denied jobs in the country's bustling defence works, and the war exposed some examples of prejudice at work. There was an occasion when black GIs, escorting German prisoners of war through the South, were refused service on railroad dining cars while their white prisoners were admitted and allowed to eat.

None the less, American blacks supported

JEEP OR PEEP?

The jeep, which went into production during World War II, took its name from the GP – general purpose – vehicle (though a lovable little character called Jeep also appeared in the Popeye comic strip). Other names were tried out, including 'blitzbuggy', 'jitterbug' and 'iron pony'. General Patton tried to popularise 'Peep', but it failed to catch on.

FEMALE TOUCH
'Rosie the Riveter' above, had counterparts among real aircraft workers.

"My girl's a WOW"
WOMAN ORDNANCE WORKER

the struggle against Nazism. Joe Louis, the world heavyweight boxing champion, told reporters: 'There may be a lot wrong in America, but there is nothing Hitler can fix.' And pressure from civil rights activists was to lead to some real advances.

For example, legislation in 1941 guaranteed blacks the jobs earlier denied in defence plants, and the number of blacks on the government payroll was to double by 1945. And the wages earned by black workers rose substantially in real terms (although, on average, their pay was still only 40 to 60 per cent of what white workers were receiving).

Altogether, the war had a hugely stimulating effect on the US economy. For ordinary people, it meant that wallets and purses were fatter than they had been for years – even if the

goods were in short supply. Wartime advertisers coped with this paradox by keeping brand names in the public eye .

Disappointed customers were told, for example, that Lucky Strike green had 'gone to war': that the manufacturers had been forced to withdraw the colour green from its packaging because the green ink had a metallic base used in aircraft production. In much the same spirit, the makers of a famous confectionery told consumers: 'If your dealer doesn't have your favorite LIFE SAVERS flavor, please be patient … It is because the shipment he would have received would have gone to the Army and Navy.'

A more aggressive note was struck by an advertisement boasting that because bomber crews had to have their intake of Vitamin C, 'maybe your canned Florida Grapefruit Juice is OVER NAZI ROOFTOPS TONIGHT!'

Production of Coca-Cola and Wrigley's chewing gum soared during the war, even though the manufacturers made negligible profits in the short term because they were supplying their products at a cut-price rate to the armed forces. The same was true of cigarettes: annual output soared from about 19 billion in 1940 to

FIGHTING MEN Joe Louis (left) meets a fellow boxer, war veteran Private Woodrow White.

HIGH FLYER A huge flag hangs between crowded tenements in New York City's Lower East Side, honouring local boys who were serving in the armed forces.

Bantam – all fitting snugly in the hand and sold at a modest price. Pocket Books could be left behind by servicemen or war workers moving from one place to another; or mailed to loved ones abroad.

Avon advertised: 'Because the new Avon books are easy to open, light to hold, thrilling to read and compact to carry or store in clothing or bags, they are ideal gifts to boys in the Armed Forces.' Dell countered with, 'BOOKS ARE WEAPONS – in a free democracy everyone may read what he likes', while Pocket Books urged its readers to 'share this book with someone in uniform'. To keep the troops entertained, people also donated paperbacks to victory book rallies nationwide.

roughly double that number in the post-war period. The popular brands – Chesterfield, Camel, Lucky Strike and so on – were hard to obtain on the home front, however, because vast quantities were being issued to troops overseas.

Paperback publishing came of age during the war years. 'Pocket Books' were sold in drug stores and on newsstands for 25 cents each. They were soon joined by rivals from Avon, Popular Library, Dell and

Madison Avenue, the heart of the American advertising trade, used every possible opportunity to sell products through war themes. One colourful magazine page, for example, showed a GI responding with delight to a letter from his wife: 'IT'S A BOY AND HE'S THRIVING ON CARNATION.' A host of other advertisements were directed at wives and girlfriends on the home front, playing on the theme of being 'lovely to come home to'. A famous soap brand, for example, suggested, 'to guard the loveliness he loves, use Palmolive.'

A DAMNED GOOD CITIZEN

Dear *Yank:*

My plane was in Los Angeles at the height of the so-called zoot-suit riots. I saw several of them and was ashamed of the servicemen involved. It must be understood, and no amount of fancy newspaper baloney can hide it, that the zoot-suit riots were really race riots, directed mainly against the Mexican, and to some degree the Negro citizens of Los Angeles. It's about time a certain element in the armed forces be told that a man can be a good American and a damned good citizen, regardless of the color of his skin, and has all the rights of a citizen. To those servicemen who took part in the riots I'd like to ask a question: What the hell uniform do you think you're wearing, American or Nazi?

Crew Chief Patterson Field, Ohio

Letter to Yank: The Army Weekly

SELLING WAR BONDS

It takes cash to fight a war – and all America's expertise in razzle-dazzle was recruited to help find funds.

TO RAISE MONEY for the national effort, the United States government issued war bonds, which were sold in banks and offices. War stamps were put on sale too, at schools, drugstores and newsstands. Costing five or ten cents, the stamps were collected especially by children who glued them into a special book which, when filled, could be traded in for a bond. Buying bonds and stamps was considered a patriotic duty, and the campaign pulled no punches: a poster of the time showed a dying GI with the legend: 'He gives his life – you only loan your money.'

Hollywood stars were recruited to promote bond sales. Comedian Jack Benny auctioned his fiddle and pin-up girl Betty Grable auctioned her stockings. Hedy Lamarr offered a personal kiss to anyone who bought a $25,000 bond, while Abbott and Costello were among those who made propaganda films explaining the principles behind the campaign.

'Hey, Abbott, what are the stamps for?'

'For defence.'

'You mean, you put the stamps on de fence? And to whom do you mail de fence?'

'You don't understand … You see, when you buy a defence stamp or defence bond you're saving your money by lending it to Uncle Sam. See, Uncle Sam needs that money to build ships and planes and tanks.'

'And what?'

'Tanks.'

'You're welcome.'

The drive to sell bonds had its casualties: Greer Garson fainted from nervous exhaustion during one drive, and Carole Lombard was killed in a plane crash while on a tour selling bonds. But the results were impressive. American families contributed $135 billion in war bonds. And they gave more still through increased taxation, which included a five per cent 'Victory Tax' added to the income revenue. On the whole, people gave willingly in the 'Taxes to beat the Axis' campaign, as they did in the war-bond drive. With higher wages and shortages of goods, there was spare cash around.

PATRIOTIC APPEAL A serviceman buys bonds from actress Evelyn Keyes in Los Angeles, 1944. Above: a poster issued in the same year when the December war-bond drive surpassed expectations, netting over $15 billion.

'TO PROMOTE A MORE PERFECT UNION...TO PROVIDE FOR THE COMMON DEFENSE

THAT WE MAY DEFEND THE LAND WE LOVE

THAT THESE MAY FACE A FUTURE UNAFRAID

THAT WE MAY PROTECT THE THINGS WE BUILD

BUY DEFENSE BONDS AND STAMPS NOW!

FOR DEFENSE BUY UNITED STATES SAVINGS BONDS

NEW YORK Views inside the giant railway station, Grand Central, were dominated by the world's largest photo mural covering the entire east wall.
Above: New Yorkers line up in May 1941 to buy Defense Stamps and Bonds on their first day of sale.

have YOU TOO bought your extra WAR BONDS?

GET ABOARD Buy VICTORY BONDS TO BRING THE BOYS Back Home Victory Loan Drive Subscribe NOW!

I'M NO MILLIONAIRE, BUT— I own a share in America
DEFENSE BONDS- STAMPS

THE PERSUADERS Posters and rallies hammered out slogans to promote sales. 'Buying war bonds was like breathing. I don't recall many people who didn't have them', recalled factory worker Shirley Hackett.

59

DEFENCE OF THE NATION

'It can happen here', warned the posters. Despite its distance from the main combat zones,

America faced real physical threat from, for example, Japanese balloon bombs and wolf packs of

German U-boats, while blackouts and air-raid drills became features of city life.

BLACKOUT curtains hung from every window of the White House in the days after Pearl Harbor, and on the front lawn a steam shovel worked around the clock to dig a trench as a bomb shelter. The staff were given gas masks and ran through air-raid drills. While an order was issued to prevent aircraft from flying over the building, gun crews were mounted on the roof.

The president himself was informed that he might have to take refuge for safety in a shelter under the treasury building. Good-naturedly, Roosevelt complained to his treasury secretary, Henry Morgenthau, that he would only go if he could, 'play poker with all the gold in your vaults'.

In the early days of the war, Americans had serious concerns that they might be the target of mass bombing raids. Trial blackouts were conducted in many American cities and an Office of Civil Defense (OCD) was set up under Fiorello La Guardia, mayor of New York, with Eleanor Roosevelt, the President's wife, as chief assistant.

All across the nation Civil Defense units were formed, often staffed by veterans of World War I who painted their service helmets white and scanned the night skies for signs of enemy aircraft. Boxes were filled with sand and buckets with water to deal with possible incendiary bombs. To help identify the different types of Japanese or German aircraft that might be sighted overhead, high school students assiduously whittled, sandpapered and glued together millions of model planes. Yet when alarms sounded immediately after Pearl Harbor, most New Yorkers simply ignored them. From more than a few blocks away, few of the sirens could be heard as anything more than the faintest mooing.

In smaller communities, air-raid drills were easier to handle. The different types of air-raid signal were identified by colour, and a typical trial blackout often began with an 'Air Raid warning – Yellow' signal. This was sounded at the local military headquarters at about nine in

FREEDOM FIGHTERS Boston youths queue to enlist on the day after Pearl Harbor. Right: Captain America battles the Axis.

HOME AND ABROAD

WHITE SILK banners with blue stars appeared in the living-room windows of city apartments and suburban houses across America during wartime. The number of stars indicated the number of loved ones in uniform, and in due course gold stars, denoting casualties, began to replace the blue ones. Along with its huge industrial output, America made a gigantic contribution to the Allied effort in human lives. Some 16 million Americans went off to fight – and 292,000 never returned.

Thousands rushed to recruiting headquarters straight after Pearl Harbor, joining queues that were sometimes several blocks long. And the really eager persisted with different branches of the services despite rejections on grounds of poor eyesight or other disabilities. Elliott Johnson, of Stockton, California, joined the marines and has recalled a friend who was rejected for being too short, 'but he

MASSACHUSETTS MOTHER A gold star flag in the window marks the death of a son, killed in action.

**STOLEN KISSES A recruit and his sweetheart kiss goodbye.
Right: the Andrews Sisters song-sheet warns against temptations.**

stayed in bed four days to put on an extra half-inch in height. His mother drove him and he laid out on the back seat all the way down there. He got on the scale and he hit the height. He was in. The Air Corps.'

The majority of servicemen were conscripts, however, and as the draft went into high gear just about every family in the country came to know what it was to have a son in uniform. Because the distances to the combat zones were so great, home leave for GIs was unusual and letters from home were vital to keep up morale.

The authorities made every effort to ensure that mail was delivered reliably. Photographs of the children were often included, and sometimes their voices were even put on gramophone records sent through the mail.

Human relations were massively disrupted none the less. The popular Andrews Sisters song *Don't Sit Under the Apple Tree* captured fighting men's real concern that their wives or girlfriends might be tempted into affairs in their absence:

*Don't sit under the apple tree
With anyone else but me
Till I come marching home*

And the lyrics also caught women's fears that their menfolk might fool around with the girls on foreign shores:

*Don't hold anyone on your knee
You'd better be true to me
You're getting the third degree
When you come marching home*

All servicemen dreaded what became known as the 'Dear John' letter, signalling the break-up of a relationship. On the home front, any woman who got pregnant while her husband was overseas became a social outcast. And if a stranger went into a bar or café with the wife or girlfriend of a local serviceman, he was looking for trouble.

BE ALERT A propaganda poster plays on fears that mass bombing could become a reality in the United States. Above: a batch of new recruits is inspected by doctors at Fort Dix, New Jersey, in 1940.

the evening, giving the Civil Defense volunteers about 15 minutes to make sure that household lights were covered or extinguished, to get ambulances ready and to have the spotters out to watch the sky. The 'Blue' warning sounded to indicate the approach of enemy aircraft and gave stragglers a last chance to prepare themselves. With the 'Red' warning – indicating enemy aircraft within ten miles – all public lighting went out and traffic was supposed to stop. While air-raid sirens wailed out their alarm, searchlights criss-crossed the night sky.

For the full effect of mass bombing, Boy Scouts daubed with blood-red tomato ketchup would lie in the streets posing as bomb victims while the ambulance teams and rescue workers rushed to their assistance.

WEST COAST ALERT

Blackout was observed with special care along the West Coast, where there were fears of Japanese invasion. Gangs sometimes prowled city streets to enforce blackout by fear if necessary. Barrage balloons loomed over key targets. People often slept in their clothes, with a packed suitcase nearby and a flashlight at hand.

Rumours that San Francisco had been bombed combined with the usual blackout accidents and confusions to create an atmosphere bordering on panic in the early months. No mass invasion occurred, but the war certainly came closer to the American mainland than many people found comfortable.

Only two months after Pearl Harbor, for example, the tanker *Montebello* was torpedoed by a Japanese

submarine within sight of the California coast. There were other sporadic incidents. On January 22, 1942, for example, a Japanese submarine shelled a military depot at Fort Stevens in Oregon. It was the first attack

SECRET WEAPON Japanese balloon bombs were launched against the United States in their thousands. Early in 1945, this one was brought down intact by the skilful flying of an American Air Force pilot. Luckily, the automatic explosion device had failed.

KEEP THE HOME FRONT PLEDGE

Pay no more than Ceiling Prices
Pay your Points in full

HELPING OUT Housewives were encouraged to honour the pricing and rationing systems. Left: sightseers tour Washington on bicycles to save gasoline.

on continental America by a foreign power since the War of 1812 when the British burned the White House. In September 1942 a light Japanese aircraft, launched by submarine, dropped incendiary bombs near Brookings, Oregon, setting a forest on fire.

Oregon also witnessed the only civilian deaths directly attributable to enemy action on US soil. The six victims – four children, a pastor and his wife – were killed by a Japanese balloon bomb.

In a six-month period beginning on November 1, 1944, the Japanese launched 9000 of these gas bags. The balloons were 33ft (10m) in diameter and designed to travel across the Pacific at a height of 30,000–35,000ft (9000–10,500m) carried by air currents travelling towards America. About one in ten of them reached the North American continent, turning up from Alaska to Mexico and bearing incendiary and fragmentation devices designed to do damage to forests, farms and cities.

DID YOU KNOW?

In 1943 the tin shortage forced Campbell's Soup to stop sponsoring the radio show *Amos 'n' Andy* after 4000 performances and 15 years on air.

The drive to collect scrap metal affected even the judiciary. In San Francisco, courts would accept a motoring offender's bumper in lieu of a cash fine.

Meat consumption in the USA actually went up during the war, despite a 28oz (795g) a week ration. This was because the government allowance permitted many poor families to eat meat regularly for the first time.

Despite the relatively small scale of the operation, the attack provoked real fears that similar devices might be used in germ warfare to shower down disease spores aimed at crops, livestock or humans. Health officers were enlisted to combat the threat and farmers were asked to report the first signs of any unusual disease in their cattle, sheep or pigs.

News of the attacks was censored, however, partly to avoid civilian panic and also to keep the Japanese from discovering that their balloons had, in fact, reached their destination. The six casualties were victims of the official silence – the children picnicking in Oregon came upon a balloon and tugged at it, exploding the bombs.

However, the voluntarily imposed press and radio blackout was so successful that in April 1945 Japan's General Kusaba, in charge of the operation, was told that he was wasting valuable resources and must shut

INTERNMENT OF THE JAPANESE

UNDER ESCORT Japanese families in Seattle are marched onto a train bound for a relocation camp in California, while friends wave goodbye.

GENERAL DWIGHT EISENHOWER, supreme commander of the Allied forces in Europe, had German ancestors. Joe DiMaggio – one of the most popular players in baseball history – was the son of Italian immigrants. No one suspected either of disloyalty to the United States during the war. In fact, there was virtually no public animosity towards people of German or Italian origin, for their communities were felt to be so well integrated into the fabric of American society that they represented no threat.

But for Japanese-Americans, things were different. The attack on Pearl Harbor and the succession of Japanese victories in 1942 provoked a craving for revenge on the home front. Hostility was particularly intense on the West Coast, where Californians feared invasion.

The Press helped to stir up a hate campaign against the one per cent of the population who were Issei (Japanese-born immigrants) or Nisei (US-born children of Issei). 'Why treat the Japs well over here?' asked a columnist. 'They take the parking positions. They get ahead of you in the stamp line at the post office. They have their share of seats on the bus and street-car lines. Let 'em be pinched, hurt, hungry, and dead up against it. Personally I hate the Japanese, and that goes for all of them.'

While newspaper cartoons daily depicted the Japanese foe in crude and sinister stereotypes, gramophone records were released with such titles as *We're Gonna Have to Slap the Dirty Little Jap,* by Lucky Millinder and his orchestra.

Signs posted in barber shop windows announced: 'JAPS SHAVED. NOT RESPONSIBLE FOR ACCIDENTS', and Japanese-Americans were refused tables in restaurants.

The persecution culminated in an official round-up of people of Japanese descent. A total of 119,803 men, women and children were held behind barbed wire at an assortment of bleak camps or relocation centres around the country. Homes, farms, businesses and furniture were confiscated. Investments and bank accounts were forfeited.

In later years the whole episode was seen as a national disgrace, and it was sharpened by the fact that 17,600 Japanese-Americans joined the army during the war – many took the oath of allegiance behind the barbed wire of their camps. They went on to serve with exceptional distinction in the European theatre of war, where the courage of their units became legendary.

THE DUTCH FIGHT ON TO VICT...

CZECHOSLOVAKS CARRY ON

We French workers warn you... defeat means slavery, starvation, death

ACROSS THE ATLANTIC
Posters reminded Americans of the struggle in occupied countries and of the likely penalties for defeat. Distanced from Nazi oppression by thousands of miles, it was easy to lose a sense of the war's purpose.

the project down: 'Your balloons are not reaching the American continent. If they were, reports would be in the newspapers. Americans could not keep their mouths closed this long.'

Off the East Coast, wolf packs of German U-boats roamed the Atlantic waters freely in the early days of the war, sinking dozens of ships in a short time. Beaches were blackened by the fuel oil spilt from wrecked tankers, and a spokesman for the oil industry warned that if the sinkings went on Americans would not be able to heat their homes or drive their cars in the winter of 1942-3. Effective anti-submarine measures eventually curtailed the menace, but not before a threat of a different kind had been revealed.

One night Coastguardsman John Cullen set out for a routine beach patrol from the Amagansett Coastguard station on Long Island, New York. A heavy fog shrouded the shoreline as he strolled along with his flashlight, to discover a small group of men hurriedly digging at the damp sand. When he challenged them, one replied by grabbing his arm and muttering: 'Here's $300 – just forget

you ever saw us, OK?' Bewildered and clutching the sheaf of bills (which in reality amounted to $240), the unarmed Cullen quickly ran back to the Coastguard station and returned with his chief within an hour. The men were gone, but in the grey haze of dawn a German submarine U202 could be seen, grounded by low tide on a sandbar, trying to free herself. From a hastily dug trench were recovered four waterproof cases packed with explosives, timing devices and detonators. Almost unbelievably, at a time when unfounded spy scares were rife, Cullen had stumbled on an authentic German sabotage team which had landed on the shores of the United States in the hopes of bringing production to a halt at various key industrial points.

The saboteurs themselves had vanished into Manhattan, but the FBI was quickly put onto the case. One of the foreign agents was to give himself up to them, turning in not only his three colleagues but another four-man team of saboteurs who were to be landed later at Ponte Vedra Beach in Florida.

YOUNG DEFENDER Boy Scouts were vital in salvage drives, held War Bond sales, worked on the land and were government dispatch-bearers too.

TOP OF THE POPS

A succession of popular songs captured the mood of the times, culminating in the first 'hit' records.

AIR-RAID SIRENS, scratchy discs and rumbling turntables were no obstacles to the enjoyment of popular music in World War II. The years of struggle produced some perennial favourites in Germany's *Lilli Marlene*, the American *I'm Dreaming of a White Christmas* and Britain's *We'll Meet Again*. Novelty hits included *The Woodpecker Song*, hugely popular on both sides of the Atlantic, though its Allied admirers may not have known that it was in origin an Italian composition which had first been published under Mussolini in 1939.

In Britain the outbreak of war was marked by a spate of patriotic songs such as *We're Gonna Hang Out the Washing on the Siegfried Line*, *There'll Always Be an England* and the jaunty *Run, Rabbit, Run!* And there was topical reference in later hits such as *Shine on Victory Moon*. But most of the great wartime favourites, hummed in factories and canteens,

HEART THROB
The French singer Maurice Chevalier serenaded Occupied France so charmingly that he was later accused of collaboration.

were songs of romantic longing and regret rather than out-and-out flag-wavers. This was true in the United States: Tin Pan Alley failed to crank up much patriotic fervour with offerings like *Let's Put the Axe in the Axis* and *You're a Sap Mr Jap*. Instead, people succumbed to *Blues in the Night*, worried that *Somebody Else is Taking My Place*, or reflected that *You'd Be So Nice to Come Home To*. And in Occupied Europe, Maurice Chevalier entertained Vichy France with songs such as *Ca Sent Si Bon La France*, extolling French virtues.

Things were changing in the music business, especially in the United States where the age of the teenage buyer and the 'hit' record was dawning. Jukeboxes played their part in the revolution. In 1939 there were 225,000 of these coin-operated machines in the United States, and by 1942 the number had risen to some 400,000 (many of them were manufactured by the Wurlitzer company). American teenagers loved the raucous sound issuing from their electrostatic speakers, and it helped to launch a clutch of young stars appealing to the bobbysoxers:

EVER POPULAR *Lilli Marlene* was one of the most popular of all the wartime hits, while Glenn Miller was awarded the first gold disc by RCA Victor, for his *Chattanooga Choo Choo*. British favourites included *We'll Meet Again*.

Frank Sinatra, for example, and Dick Haymes (famous for his rendering of *You'll Never Know*). The new idols were not great favourites with the GIs, however. Sinatra, in particular, incurred some dislike among servicemen – and not just because he made

LATEST TECHNOLOGY The RCA Victrola promised improved sound combined with the ability to stack and play several records.

Billboard published its first 'Music Popularity Chart' on July 20, 1940. *I'll Never Smile Again*, by Tommy Dorsey (with vocalist Frank Sinatra), was the first ever 'Number One' record. It became every artist's aim to sell more than a million records, an achievement crowned by the presentation of a gold disc – another innovation of the war years.

No hit could last more than two or three minutes for there were no long-playing records in World War II. Discs were played at a speed of 78 rpm, and any extended piece of music – a complete opera, for instance – called for a whole stack of records which were usually changed by hand. Auto-change gramophones did exist, taking stacks of 20 or more discs at a time, but for the wartime music-lover listening to a long piece still involved repeated interruptions as disc after disc dropped with a clunk into the playing position.

Wealthier families, meanwhile, listened to their favourite Bing Crosby or Duke Ellington records on all-electric gramophones that had loudspeaker amplification. Radio grams were available, too, combining the record player with a wireless. But the old wind-up portable with its horn – so popular in the trench dugouts of World War I – had not entirely disappeared. The gramophone was often referred to as the Victrola, after one of the vintage makes which were still very much in evidence, and sound quality was poor by present-day standards.

All records were pressed on shellac, a brittle material easily scratched and worn by the steel needles of the time. Recording methods had their limitations, and although new techniques evolved during the war, they came too late for the ordinary music-lover. The first High-Fidelity discs (issued by the English company Decca) appeared in December 1944, but it was another year before Hi-Fi gramophones appeared. And listeners would have to wait until 1948 for long-playing (LP) microgroove records, made of the 'unbreakable' plastic, Vinylite.

the girls back home swoon. 'The Voice', as he was often known, had escaped the draft because of a weak heart.

Repeated playings of a song on the drugstore jukebox – and repeated requests on wartime radio shows – helped to seal the idea of the hit record in the public mind. Even before war broke out, an American radio show called Hit Parade was presenting the top-selling tunes of the week. It remained a favourite programme during World War II, and the practice of listing top sellers was continued when the magazine

HIT PARADE Jukeboxes, such as this Wurlitzer model, quickly became popular in the United States and helped to create the first 'hit' records.

HOLLYWOOD AT WAR

'You can tell by the cast it's important! gripping! big!' ran the publicity for the screen classic *Casablanca*. Whether Humphrey Bogart, Errol Flynn, Donald Duck or Sherlock Holmes was involved, when Hollywood went to war it made sure that the whole world knew about it.

IN THE 1940s Hollywood was still the dream factory of the Western world, and at the outbreak of war it was turning out more than 500 films a year. Some 17,000 motion picture theatres in the United States offered one seat for every 12 American men, women and children. Admission charges ran from $2.20 for first showings in the big city theatres down to as little as 10 cents in farm districts and the cheap urban cinemas.

Some 85 million Americans were happy to pay for a seat each week, and in a pre-television age the choice was not which channel to watch, but 'Shall we go to the Majestic or the Bijou?' The big picture was not the only attraction. An evening's entertainment also took in the B movie (a low-budget supporting film) with additional shorts, cartoons and newsreels.

The war brought a heightened interest in current affairs, and theatres devoted entirely to newsreels suddenly emerged in America's big cities. Fox Movietone had the biggest distribution, and the voice of its top commentator, Lowell Thomas, helped to bring the war's events to millions of cinema-goers.

Documentaries played an important role too. Soon after Pearl Harbor top Hollywood directors were

TIMELY TALE *Mrs Miniver* described English family life under the Blitz. Two young honeymooners (above) view the destruction of the Miniver home.

Greer GARSON Walter PIDGEON in MRS. MINIVER

"It's Vin's plane... he's signalling to us... he's safely back!"

called upon to produce documentary films explaining the war and the need to defeat the Axis powers. One of these directors was Frank Capra, who became head of the War Department's film section. Capra went on to make a celebrated series called *Why We Fight* with such titles as *The Nazis Strike* (1943), *The Battle of Britain* (1943) and *War Comes to America* (1944).

The first American combat film was *The Battle of Midway* (1942) made by John Ford, then serving with the US Navy. Though wounded, Ford kept his camera rolling to produce a 20-minute classic that won an Academy Award. Another Ford masterpiece was *The Battle of San Pietro* (1944), a moving documentary made during the Italian campaign about a midwinter action. The camera, shaken sometimes by bombardment, showed close-up footage of fighting; the slow advance of US patrols creeping from house to house; and the return of local people to their devastated homes.

WARTIME THEMES

Almost every week there were new releases of short films about the national struggle. There was *Tanks,* for example, a short on tank production with commentary by Orson Welles, and *Get the Scrap* by Walt Disney, about conserving raw materials. War themes were picked up in cartoons. Donald Duck appeared in a high-spirited item called *Der Führer's Face,* and the title song proved very popular – though it was never played on the radio because of the ribald innuendo in the lyrics.

The B movies themselves had passionate fans in many small-town audiences who often preferred them to the main feature. Their action was crisp and their morality uncomplicated

The B-movie serials also had keen devotees: fans of the Lone Ranger, Charlie Chan, Flash Gordon or the girl reporter Torchy Blaine could not bear to miss an episode, and after Pearl Harbor war themes entered these supporting films too. For example, *Sherlock*

HOLLYWOOD HOSTESSES Film star Marlene Dietrich joins Mrs Thomas F. Sullivan in serving coffee to GIs at the Hollywood Canteen. Mrs Sullivan lost her five sons aboard the cruiser *Juneau,* and a wartime film was based on the brothers' lives.

PRESIDENTIAL ADDRESS Roosevelt appeared on this advertisement, unveiled in Times Square. The United Service Organization enlisted stars for the war effort.

Holmes and the Secret Weapon (1942) had the immortal detective, played by Basil Rathbone, pitted against Nazi saboteurs. And even the *Invisible Man,* played by Jon Hall, entered the lists for democracy, parachuting into Berlin in *The Invisible Agent* (1942). Tarzan and Lassie, too, both did their bit for the war.

But besides the welter of low-budget productions, wartime Hollywood came up with many more substantial offerings. One of these was *Mrs Miniver* (1942), directed by William Wyler, with Greer Garson as the heroine and Walter Pidgeon as her husband. This was a sincere attempt by Hollywood to pay tribute to the courage and sacrifice of British people by focusing on one ordinary middle-class family. Set in a rose-strewn English village of the dreamy Hollywood variety, the film faced criticism even in its own day for its stereotyped rural characters and lapses into melodrama (the family faces everything – including a German parachutist). Yet the film also stirred very deep emotions, strengthening morale in Britain and doing much to make ordinary American families feel for the plight of their British counterparts. 'Just saw *Mrs Miniver*,' wrote the author Eric Knight. 'It stinks. It's tremendous. It's hogwash. It makes people cheer … Oh God, these Hollywood men with their funny ideas of what this war's about!'

By no means all of the big films enjoyed on the home front had themes connected with the war. Many audiences, fretting over ration books and casualty lists, wanted the glamorous escapism of musicals like *My Gal Sal* (1942) and *Meet Me in St Louis* (1944) starring the young Judy Garland. Disney's superb feature-length cartoon *Bambi* (1942) was a product of the time, as was the classic thriller

CLASSIC THRILLER
Barbara Stanwyck,
Fred MacMurray
and Edward G.
Robinson star in
Double Indemnity,
one of the great
films noirs, made
in 1944.

Double Indemnity (1944) with Fred MacMurray and Barbara Stanwyck.

War films drew large audiences. Action movies included *Desperate Journey* (1942) starring Errol Flynn as one of three POWs in Nazi Germany fighting their way to freedom ('Now for Australia and a crack at those Japs!' is Flynn's exuberant last line).

Wake Island, made in the same year, described the struggle of marines to defend a small Pacific island against Japanese attack. It was harder and more terse than Flynn's offering; *Newsweek* called it 'Hollywood's first intelligent, honest and completely

successful attempt to dramatise the deeds of an American force on a fighting front'.

Later on came *The Story of GI Joe* (1945), a poignant portrayal of real-life war correspondent Ernie Pyle, played by Burgess Meredith, as he lived and marched with combat troops in Italy. Pyle was an enormously popular journalist whose wartime reports were syndicated in about 300 newspapers in the United States. He died in April 1945, falling in the Pacific to a Japanese sniper's bullet.

And then, in 1942, there

BANDSMEN
Frank Sinatra
sings with the
Tommy Dorsey
Band. Inset: the
great wartime
bandleaders
Benny Goodman
(left) and Glenn
Miller, creator of
In the Mood and
*Moonlight
Serenade.*

WARTIME RADIO

FIRESIDE CHAT
President Roosevelt delivers one of his famous broadcasts. Above: a Pennsylvania family listens as the President speaks.

THROUGHOUT AMERICA, countless families were to experience the war more than anything else as a series of radio programmes. The average listener spent four hours a day at the wireless set.

President Roosevelt himself proved a superb radio speaker through his famous 'fireside chats' broadcast from the White House. They had begun on March 12, 1933, and were marked by an intimate

COMMENTATOR Ed Murrow was CBS radio correspondent in London during the Blitz.

approach wholly different from the radio bombast of Hitler and Mussolini, or the stirring solemnities of Winston Churchill.

The radios of the day were big, heavy, wood-panelled affairs, but not very powerful. People had to sit near the set with someone fiddling at the knobs to make sure that the crackling voice came through.

The voice of Edward R. Murrow also became familiar to millions. In August 1940, at the height of the Battle of Britain, CBS radio started his *London After Dark* series which helped ordinary Americans to understand what war really meant in beleaguered Britain. Later, he would be heard broadcasting from a B-17 Flying Fortress on a bombing raid over Berlin.

In February 1942 came the 13-week series *This Is War*. With titles like 'The Enemy', 'America at War', 'Your Army' and so on, broadcast nationwide every

Saturday night, it had the overt purpose of inspiring or even frightening people into the national struggle. The OWI (Office of War Information) also produced radio appeals to save fat and collect tinfoil; exhortations to dig Victory gardens; appeals for glider pilots to volunteer for the air force; and so on.

The radio was also, of course, a great source of entertainment. The wisecracks of Red Skelton, Jimmy Durante, Burns and Allen, Abbott and Costello, Bob Hope and others all helped to keep spirits up.

In popular music the wartime years were, above all, the years of swing and the big bands. *In the Mood,* played by Glenn Miller's American Air Force Band, was one of the great wartime tunes, along with the equally memorable *Moonlight Serenade.* His unique sound, with its saxophones and muted brass, acquired a special poignancy when, in December 1944, his plane went missing on a routine flight from England to France.

TROOP REVUE **This is the Army,** concerning recruits who put on a musical, was filmed on the world's biggest sound stage. Right: composer Irving Berlin makes a personal appearance.

was *Casablanca*. If any movie united all the best elements of Hollywood film-making in wartime it was surely this Humphrey Bogart classic. Romance, suspense, humour and intrigue were all mixed in a wartime setting. There was even music, in the form of the haunting *As Time Goes By*, sung by bar pianist Dooley Wilson.

DID YOU KNOW?

In the Hollywood classic *Casablanca*, Humphrey Bogart is often quoted as saying 'Play it again, Sam' to his pianist. In reality, Bogart never makes the remark. The line is, 'Play it, Sam', and it is delivered by the heroine, played by Ingrid Bergman.

The sum of $8000 in damages was awarded to a young starlet against the Hollywood Canteen after she injured her spine while dancing with a 'jive-maddened' marine. Jitterbugging presented a real danger, the judge said in summing up, 'to one not skilled or expert in it'.

The setting is Rick's Café in French Morocco where refugees from occupied Europe assemble while waiting to get hold of exit visas. Bogart plays the hard-boiled café owner who forsakes his cynicism to help an old love flee to freedom with her Resistance leader husband. Ingrid Bergman is the leading lady, Peter Lorre the petty racketeer holding the all-important letters of transit, and Conrad Veidt plays Major Strasser, the menacing German officer. The film has always exerted a fascination. It was as if Rick served as a metaphor for the American character: tough-minded, isolationist, yet capable of heroic self-sacrifice. The fate of free Europe, the film seemed to imply, depended on how the American would act.

ENTERTAINING THE TROOPS

Offscreen, the job of entertaining servicemen was done by the USO (United Service Organization). A host of Hollywood stars participated in its troop concerts both overseas and on the home front, and many detected a strong, no-nonsense attitude in their audience. The war was rough, recruits felt, and it had to be endured – but too much high-minded talk about the defence of democracy did not go down well.

Edward G. Robinson, entertaining American airmen at one base, had an awkward moment. 'I began by saying: "I am happy to be here, the most privileged moment of my life, to see the men who are defeating Hitler." I have never laid so big a bomb in my life. I could sense the audience despising me. So that crazy actor instinct took over, and to stop the buzz of their boos and Bronx cheers, I ad-libbed, "Pipe down, you mugs, or I'll let you have it. Whaddya hear from the mob?" There was an instant burst of high laughter and applause.'

The cartoonist Bill Mauldin, with his tough and grimy soldier characters Willie and Joe, caught the same attitude in a famous cartoon. 'Just gimme a coupla aspirin,' says the GI, turning down a medal. 'I already got a Purple Heart.' And Bob Hope, one of the most indefatigable troop entertainers, took risks with his gags even when visiting wounded servicemen in hospital. Entering the wards lined with injured men, he would call out: 'Did you see our show, or were you sick before?' To a room full of GIs in traction he once remarked, 'OK, fellas, don't get up!'

The hospital visits could be harrowing for the stars themselves. Maxene Andrews of the famous Andrews Sisters spoke movingly of a visit to Oak Knoll Hospital in San Francisco, then full of troops wounded in the Solomon Islands. She and her sisters sang for three hours among the beds of the bandaged and disfigured and as they were leaving a male nurse came over to them saying that he had a young patient who would love to hear them sing.

'We went down a long, long hallway and stopped in front of a door that two male nurses were guarding. We were ushered in. We were in a padded cell. The two guards closed the door behind us. We were alone.

'In the corner, we saw a figure facing the wall. We started to sing *Apple Blossom Time*. About halfway through, we began to hear this hum. It was discordant and got louder and louder. When we came to the end of the song, we didn't stop. We just kept singing. We repeated it and repeated it. The figure turned around. He couldn't have been more than nineteen years old. His eyes were looking at us, but he wasn't seeing us. He was lost in another world. He was just humming and humming. He was so handsome and so young.'

Not all encounters between the stars and servicemen were so grim. On Broadway there emerged one of the biggest wartime news-makers, the

YOU MUST REMEMBER THIS The airport farewell from *Casablanca*. As Ingrid Bergman leaves with her husband, Paul Henreid, Bogart reflects, 'The problems of three little people don't amount to a hill of beans in this crazy world ...'

STAR TURNS
Mary Pickford opens an army canteen; Cary Grant and other stars (right) assemble for a Washington benefit concert.

famous Stage Door Canteen, which opened in March 1942 in the basement of the Forty-fourth Street Theatre specifically to entertain members of the armed services. Everything was free for the soldiers, sailors and airmen who packed the house from 9pm until the midnight closing time. Showbusiness personalities turned up nightly to do their turns, while starlets were hired as Canteen hostesses, expected to dance with any servicemen who asked, to serve them drinks or coffee, and to listen to their stories. A Stage Door Canteen was set up in Hollywood, too, and opened in November by Bette Davis and John Garfield. Judy Garland was among those waiting on tables, while Betty Grable danced with the customers.

Back in the theatres on Broadway, wartime hits included Irving Berlin's splendid army show *This Is the Army*, with an all-military cast except for one man: the composer himself. But perhaps the biggest event was the debut of *Oklahoma* – by Richard Rodgers and Oscar Hammerstein, which opened on March 31, 1943, and went on to beat all existing records for a musical.

Another showbusiness sensation on the home front was a frail and pale-faced crooner called Francis Albert Sinatra, who shot to stardom in the summer of 1942. Already in his mid-twenties, Sinatra could have been mistaken for a teenager and he was a smash hit with the bobby sox generation of high school kids. Girls screamed and swooned at his concerts. Autograph hunters pursued him wherever he went. Two thousand Frankie fan clubs sprang up around the country while The Voice, as he was known, became a multi-millionaire. An older generation of music lovers was bewildered. When someone told Bing Crosby that a voice like Sinatra's came only once in a lifetime, Bing quipped: 'Sure, but why does it have to be in my lifetime?'

HOPE FOR VICTORY   Comedian Bob Hope entertains troops in the Solomons. A wartime survey made him the biggest box-office draw after pin-up Betty Grable.

THE WARTIME CHRISTMAS

With families separated, toy shops empty and trees unlit, millions

yearned for a Christmas 'just like the ones we used to know'.

THE WORLD'S second most popular Christmas song (after *Silent Night*) was recorded in wartime. *White Christmas* sung by Bing Crosby featured in the 1942 screen smash *Holiday Inn* and American cinema audiences in that first year cheered the song until they were hoarse. Its astonishing success left even the songwriter, Irving Berlin, bewildered. 'It came out at a time when we were at war, and it became a peace song in wartime – a meaning I never intended,' he said later.

To millions who went through World War II the very idea of Christmas developed a special poignance, recalling lost worlds of domestic content, faraway homes or faraway loved ones – and an equally faraway spirit of goodwill. The festival was celebrated with all the little extravagances available, as if to defy the bombs, the shortages and the baleful eyes of authorities who continually exhorted people to be more thrifty. In the United States, for example, Hollywood child star Margaret O'Brien was photographed enjoying an Austerity Christmas beside an unlit Christmas tree hung with Savings Bonds and Stamps instead of toys. In Australia government minister John Dedman banned any mention of Christmas in advertising during December 1942, and his crusade against wasteful expense earned him the name of 'The Man Who Killed Father Christmas'.

In beleaguered Britain, carol singers were told not to ring bells in case they were confused with air-raid signals. Midnight Mass was cancelled in some churches because of the difficulties in blacking out huge stained glass windows. The traditional oranges and nuts vanished from the toes of Christmas stockings; Christmas poultry was generally available only through the black market and carrots took the place of dried fruit in millions of Christmas puddings.

Toy factories had been taken over for munitions production, so that 'Wanted' and 'For Sale' notices in the newspapers crowded columns with requests or advertisements for secondhand items. In John Lewis's bombed-out Oxford Street store in London, tents were erected to celebrate a Potato Christmas Fair sponsored by the Ministry of Food's propaganda figure, Potato Pete. Here dutiful children received hot baked potatoes, pledging: 'I promise as my Christmas gift to the sailors who have to bring us our bread that I will do all I can to eat home-grown potatoes instead.'

Throughout Europe there were people enduring Christmas without gas, water or electricity; some as

DECK THE HALLS
Britons celebrate in
an Anderson shelter.

Boldog karácsonyi ünnepeket

YULETIDE 1939
A Hungarian postcard shows
Christmas in jeopardy.

TUNED IN A Christmas broadcast in France. Left: A US terminus.

refugees and some in the bomb-blasted shells of their own homes. For many, the splitting up of families was the worst feature of wartime Christmas, with husbands in the armed forces, children evacuated, wives and girlfriends doing farm or factory work far from home.

Then there was the cold. Parisians who survived the Occupation remembered the ferocious winters as among the worst features of the war, especially December 1940, before a black market had been properly organised. The Germans had seized all supplies of coal, so that fireplaces were empty and people went straight to bed after supper. The occupiers had stripped the shops of toys, furs, perfumes, jewellery and fancy lingerie to send home for their wives and families. Drue Tartière, an American-born Parisian woman, recalled how in 1942: 'The German women in the Nazi women's corps whom one saw in the Métro were carrying gaily wrapped bundles and miniature Christmas trees. Every German soldier and his girl seemed to have packages tied with gay ribbons. The French snarled at them and shivered in their shabby, worn clothing.'

Yet people managed to celebrate Christmas with little luxuries, even in the most difficult circumstances. Anne Frank, the Jewish girl hiding with her parents and others in the sealed-off back room of an Amsterdam office recorded in her diary for December 1943 how gifts were brought by their Dutch helpers. 'Miep had made a lovely Christmas cake, on which was written "Peace 1944". Ellie had provided a pound of sweet biscuits of pre-war quality. For Peter, Margot and me a bottle of Yoghurt, and a bottle of beer for the grown-ups. Everything was so nicely done up, and there were pictures stuck on the different parcels.'

Germany itself suffered hardships, especially in 1944 when the flow of luxuries – fancy goods from France, bacon, lard and geese from Poland and so on – had dried up. When the radio blared propaganda, carols and Beethoven, bombed-out families and stumbling, half-frozen refugees from the east received food rations at the bare survival level. Still, the scraps of decoration went up, *Stille Nacht* was sung and prayers were offered for the dead and the missing. Christmas represented continuity with the past – and with traditions more enduring than those of Hitler's disintegrating Reich.

RATIONING AND RESTRICTIONS

'I spent a lot of time standing in line. So many things were rationed, coffee and sugar and flour,

that any time you would see a line you would automatically get in it'

— Esther Burgard, housewife.

W HEN DEPRIVATION came, the first thing people noticed was the shortage of rubber. The buying of tyres was banned or strictly limited (as was the purchase of other rubber goods such as hot-water bottles, beach balls, rubber floor mats and garden hoses). In response, people improvised as best they could – by recapping or retreading old tyres, for example. The term 'retread' became one of the catchwords of the time, used not only of reconditioned tyres but of a worn-out combat soldier who was sent back on active service.

It was largely to save tyres that gasoline rationing was introduced from December 1, 1942. Throughout North America, the transport restrictions became a real annoyance. An ordinary citizen received a black 'A' windshield sticker entitling him or her to buy three gallons a week – about 60 miles of driving in the fuel-hungry automobiles of the day. People were asked to share rides, too. 'When you ride ALONE you ride with Hitler!' warned a poster of the time, showing a spectral Führer sitting beside a motorist.

As a result, the highways became more and more deserted. The railroads, in contrast, faced massive overcrowding, as did other forms of public transportation. The bus now became the great symbolic vehicle of the American home front, packed with passengers and often running late. Servicemen knew it as the only means of getting from camp to town for entertainment, and on nights when not much was happening the lonely hours spent in and around desolate bus stations became for many GIs their most enduring memory of wartime boredom.

People walked a lot too, though this caused problems of its own. Shoe rationing began in February 1943, civilians being limited to two pairs a year so that even the better-off resorted to half-soling. As for clothing, the government slogan ran:

Use it up, wear it out
Make it do, or do without.

Save waste fats for explosives

TAKE THEM TO YOUR MEAT DEALER

YOUR SCRAP ...brought it down

KEEP SCRAPPING Rubber·Metal·Rags

GIVE TO A COLLECTOR, SALVAGE DEPOT OR SELL TO A DEALER

SCRAPPING Thousands of posters exhorted people to save waste material for the war effort.

We Are Ready ★ What About You?
Join the
SCHOOLS AT WAR *Program*

SPONSORED BY : THE WAR SAVINGS STAFF OF THE U. S. TREASURY DEPARTMENT, THE U. S. OFFICE OF EDUCATION AND ITS WARTIME COMMISSION

Clothing was rationed by the War Production Board, which also placed a limit on the amount of fabric that could be used for a man's suit. The so-called L-35 edict ended the zoot-suit craze of the early war years, when youths calling themselves 'hepcats' went around in outsize jackets and huge, baggy trousers. For the complete effect, the zoot-suiter also sported a wide-brimmed hat and a long chain dangling from his belt. The flamboyance provoked hostility. In 1943 there were 'zoot-suit riots' in which GIs beat up Hispanic and black youths sporting the clothes.

FASHIONS FOR THE WARTIME WOMAN

Deprivation hit women's fashions too. People spoke of 'bottled' or 'liquid' stockings – legs were painted with one or another staining preparation – and as in Europe, American girls grew accustomed to drawing pretend 'seams' with dark eyebrow pencils down the backs of their bare legs. The first brands of nylon stockings had been launched in the United States in May 1940, and proved enormously popular. They were hit, however, by the war need for nylon as a

POTATO LINE Queuing became a habit. A woman recalls, 'My little boy would ask, "Mother, what are we standing in line for now?" and I'd say, "I don't know, but we'll soon find out".'

parachute material, and nylon stockings became obtainable only on the black market, where they sold for $5 a pair.

After rationing began, skirts rose several inches above the knee, with minimal pleats and no zippers (the metal was needed by the military). In vain did the fashion gurus of the day try to encourage little feminine frivolities to soften the new, austere look. The Government opposed a move to reintroduce frilly underwear, provoking South Carolina's Senator 'Cotton Ed' Smith to fume in the Senate: 'How in the hell are you gonna win the war by taking the ruffles out of

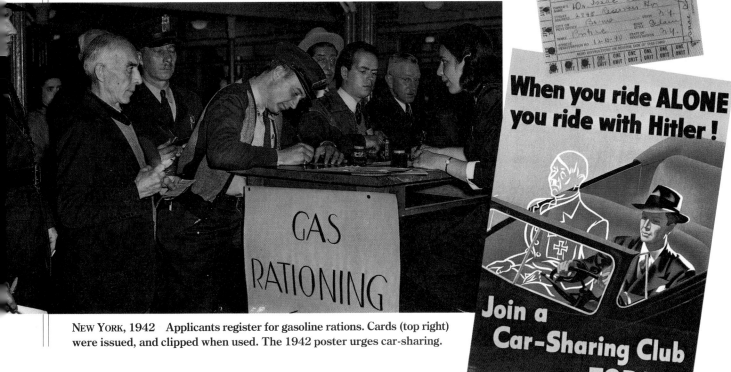

NEW YORK, 1942 Applicants register for gasoline rations. Cards (top right) were issued, and clipped when used. The 1942 poster urges car-sharing.

THE CHILDREN'S WAR

In the world of children's comics, an assortment of heroes helped to defeat the enemy, and children were exhorted to 'do their bit'.

IN DECEMBER 1941, only a few hours after Japan's surprise attack on Pearl Harbor, Walt Disney received a telephone call at his home, informing him that US Army units had occupied his Hollywood studio. Ignoring cries of protest from his employees, they had driven straight to the main sound stage, thrown out the film recording equipment, and turned the area into a repair shop for their trucks and guns. An ammunition dump was set up in the studio's car park, and other buildings became dormitories for the troops. The reason for the upheaval, Disney was told, was the military's need for a suitable base from which they could protect southern California from a possible Japanese invasion.

The war penetrated every aspect of life – even the dream factory that had given the world's children such classics as *Snow White and the Seven Dwarfs* and *Pinocchio*. Soldiers occupied Disney's studio for seven months in all, and the film-maker was obliged to abandon three major cartoon

RELAXING WITH MOTHER The enduring popularity of children's comics as a source of entertainment secured a captive audience.

features to make propaganda shorts for the government.

Among these, however, was yet another classic, the superb Donald Duck caper *Der Führer's Face*, boasting one novelty song that was to be hugely relished by small boys on both sides of the Atlantic. Its chief appeal lay in the opportunities it provided for them to blow raspberries (or 'Bronx cheers', as they were known in the

United States) at various appropriate points in the lyrics:

Ven der Führer says
'Ve iss der Master Race'
Ve Heil! (raspberry)
Heil! (raspberry)
Right in der Führer's face.

At home and in their schoolyards alike, young Americans pored over Action Comic

COMING TO THE RESCUE With the outbreak of war, boys' comics were filled with stories of the daring exploits of a variety of heroes in the fight against Germany.

adventures showing Superman baring his knuckles at the Nazi foe. In Britain, war themes entered the boys' papers: the *Adventure*, the *Rover*, the *Wizard* and the *Skipper*, where German spies, secret codes and invisible ink were staple fare in many tales. The *Hotspur* carried stories about a mythical public school, Red Circle, where the popular sports master was called away on Secret Service work. Young readers fought back the tears when he was killed off some weeks later.

Toys were scarce in wartime, but it was possible to find such

ONGOING ATTRACTION The cartoon favourite Tintin embarks on another of his adventures, which continued throughout the war.

items as 'The Mystic Dancing Illusion Models', a cut-out dancing figure that showed Adolf Hitler on the front – and his skeleton on the back. In comics, Axis leaders were usually turned into figures of fun. In Britain, for example, the much-loved comic *Beano* had Hitler and Goering portrayed as Addie

WINNERS ALL *Beano's* unlikely hero wins the day while the boys of *Hotspur's* Red Circle school make their contribution to victory.

and Hermy – the Nasty Nazis 'Himmel! Der pig-dog British are saving all their waste paper!' they would cry in alarm as they scanned the embattled island through their magic telescopes. Against the deadly duo were pitted Lord Snooty and his pals, Pansy Potter and Desperate Dan. Readers also were vouchsafed AMAZING PICTURES FROM GERMANY. HITLER AND GOERING CHASED BY MONSTER WASP! ('Ha! Ha! Willy the Wasp's cut up rough in Germany. Ten thousand Jerry soldiers in hospital. That'll teach 'em').

The *Beano's* favourite figure of fun, however, was Musso da Wop – 'he's a big-a-da-flop'. His bungling generals were capable of every kind of stupidity, even supplying their troops with spaghetti for bootlaces. The *Beano* also put a few riddles before its readers. 'Why does Musso never change his socks?' asked one. 'Because he smells defeat.' Fearing that readers might fail to spot the pun, the editors took the precaution of adding 'de feet' in brackets.

The war was not always presented to children in such frivolous terms. In Allied and Axis countries alike, publications for the young also contained uplifting exhortations to 'Do Your Bit', along with surveys of 'Our Wonderful Fighting Forces' and morale-boosting articles with titles such as 'Why We Cannot Lose'. And there were plenty of contributors, too, who simply carried on regardless, penning their usual escapist fare about assorted footballing heroes, schoolgirl detectives, jungle explorers

SUPERHEROES American heroes race to the service of their country while Wonder Woman overruns the German trenches.

and prairie queens as if there was no war at all.

This was the wisest policy in the occupied nations – though it was no guarantee of long-term popularity. In occupied Belgium, the author and illustrator Hergé (real name Georges Remi) continued to publish his Tintin adventures; classics such as *The Secret of the Unicorn* and *Red Rackham's Treasure* were products of the war years. After the liberation, however, Hergé was dubbed a collaborator. In 1992 a former SS officer claimed that Tintin, the teenage reporter with his plus fours and upswept quiff, was delivering a pro-Nazi message.

THIRST FOR NEWS Children in Britain and America pored over their comics for the latest news of their favourite characters.

POINTS TO WATCH Processed foods were bought on a points system of rationing. A tin of soup, for example, was six points, sliced pineapple was 24 points while baby foods were only one or two points. Preserving home-grown produce (right) yielded ration-free food.

"We'll have lots to eat this winter, won't we Mother?"

**Grow your own
Can your own**

ladies' lingerie?' The authorities even ordered a 10 per cent reduction in the quantity of cloth going into women's bathing suits. The order finally killed the bathing skirts of earlier times, and encouraged two-piece rather than one-piece costumes.

For convenience, many working women took to wearing slacks. By the summer of 1942 it was reported that sales of women's trousers were five times what they had been the year before, and the trend was to endure. Styles picked up wartime themes: there was a vogue for wearing patches on knees, elbows and back-sides, for example, alluding to the need to 'make do'.

Among the younger generation, the new vogue was for casual, boyish clothes. High school girls, known as 'bobby soxers' after their short cotton socks, took to wearing flat-soled loafers, Sloppy Joe sweaters and blue jeans.

Because metals were needed for the war effort, an astonishing range of household and other goods vanished from the shops, and huge government drives were mounted to collect every-thing from aluminium utensils to toothpaste tubes.

'Slap the Jap with Scrap!' and 'Hit Hitler with the Junk!' ran the drive to salvage steel. The campaign brought in everything from hand-fuls of rivets to a hunk of the USS *Maine,* an American battleship dredged up from Havana harbour where she had been sunk in 1898. Scrap rubber was salvaged too, in the form of worn tyres, gumboots and even floor mats from automobiles.

The very texture of everyday life changed in war-time America, as people got used to handling books and newspapers printed on grey paper so cheap and coarse that bits of twig could sometimes be discerned in it. Kleenex was practically unobtainable, and toilet paper scarce.

Food rationing started a month after Pearl Harbor, and sugar was the first commodity to be controlled. It was not long before candy and chewing gum became hard for civilians to obtain. Coffee, butter, cheese, canned goods and meat were later rationed. People accustomed them-selves more and more to the tastes of Spam and margarine (a butter substitute). Rabbit often appeared on dinner tables in place of beef; macaroni and cheese became a staple dish; tuna casserole surprise became anything but surprising; and a can of corned beef was thought a treat in many families.

STYLE WAR A zoot-suiter with his 'hep chick'. The attire provoked hostility from GIs and the War Production Board.

ON THE TRACKS

IN AN AGE when the hit song *Chattanooga-Choo-Choo* celebrated the wonders of transcontinental rail travel, America's rail network faced awesome problems of overcrowding. It has been estimated that during the 44 months when the USA was at war, 113,891 special troop-trains moved an average of nearly a million servicemen a month. An immense effort was made by volunteer organisations such as the Salvation Army, the Red Cross and the Boy Scouts to help entertain the travelling servicemen by bringing baskets of books, magazines and jigsaw puzzles to hand out at the railroad stations.

It was all hugely inconvenient for the ordinary civilian passengers, of course. But griping was discouraged by what became one of the most famous advertisements of the war. This was 'The Kid in Upper 4'.

The illustration showed a scene on a troop train at 3.42am. The young soldier in the top berth is wide awake, remembering the things he is leaving behind as he goes to war: 'The taste of hamburgers and pop ... The feel of driving a roadster over a six-lane highway ... A dog named Shucks, or Spot, or Barnacle Bill.' As he thinks them over, 'There's a lump in his throat. And maybe – a tear fills his eye. It doesn't matter, Kid. Nobody will see ... It's too dark.'

The advertisement was put out by the New Haven Railroad to ward off complaints from civilian users. If the corridors were packed and there was standing room only, if there was a shortage of berths or of seats in the diner, passengers were asked to remember the Kid in Upper 4 – and make no fuss.

The railway system had been developed largely in the decades after the Civil War and, although it had done good service during World War I, it had suffered neglect during the years of the Depression. War

STREAMLINED SELLING
In 1942 the latest Union Pacific locomotive rolls from the sheds to become a mobile red, white and blue poster for war bonds.

with Japan and Germany, moreover, required shipments to the East and West Coasts simultaneously (in World War I all the traffic had been eastbound).

With its huge freight of passengers, the scene was set for disaster. In 1943 especially, it seemed that hardly a month passed without a train crash.

One result was a Senate investigating committee which called for an urgent increase in the production of track, freight and passenger cars to prevent the total collapse of the wartime transportation system. Another was that the authorities permitted several lines to start using diesel-driven engines. So it was that the romantic era of the steam-powered 'iron horse' drew towards its close. It was in wartime that the green, diesel-driven engines first started to move along American tracks.

TROOP TRAIN Millions destined for army, naval and air bases strained railways to the limit.

'HOME-FRONT MOBILISATION'
WARTIME CHICAGO

There was the constant idea that you had to be doing something to help. It did filter down to the neighborhood: home-front mobilization. We had a block captain. It was always some goof who wanted somethin' like that, who could become a little official fellow. A sort of neighborhood guy who nobody would have ever noticed under normal circumstances. But he had his white helmet. He was the air-raid warden. The siren would go off and everybody would turn off the lights. He would go around the neighborhood banging on doors and yelling, "Your lights are on". He'd write down people's names if they had a little light on in their apartments. I didn't like this. My parents were downstairs, running the tavern, so I'd have to turn out these damn lights. My brother and I would sit there in this absolutely pitch-black apartment. We were afraid that if we didn't, the air-raid warden would come by and the FBI would come and terrible things would happen. I remember the guy because he was later arrested on some child-molesting charge. He was the neighborhood creep.

From the recollections of Mike Royko, Chicago columnist.

People retained mouth-watering memories from better days, however. In one broadcast entertainment, comedian Bob Hope answered a request from a pair of GIs: 'Please have Lana Turner come out and fry us a three-inch porterhouse steak smothered with onions – and let's hear it sizzle.' The steak was brought forth under armed guard and cooked by the film beauty while millions listened, drooling, at their radios.

People grew their own fruit and vegetables. By

BOBBY SOXERS Sporting the short cotton socks that gave them their name, these girls helping with farmwork also wear the latest fashion item: blue jeans.

1943 America's 20 million Victory gardens were supplying a third of the country's fresh vegetables, spurred on by such slogans as 'Backyard radishes can hasten the homecoming!' Beer was watered down and there was a whisky drought from the autumn of 1942 to the summer of 1944, when inveterate drinkers made do with the likes of Olde Spud, a whisky substitute distilled from waste potatoes and skins.

There were shortages of just about everything: vast quantities of cigarettes went to the troops, and with the blackout, flashlights fell into short supply, and people had to line up for candles. World maps disappeared from the shelves, as people bought them in their thousands to follow the course of the war in the Pacific, North Africa and Europe.

In 1945, January 15 was declared a 'dim-out' day for the whole United States to try and combat the shortage of fuel.

And housing, above all, was in short supply. With the flood of war workers to urban centres, the pressure on accommodation was acute. Householders in some wartime boom towns became used to finding new arrivals, with their rolled bedding, camping out in their backyards or on their front porches. In Los Angeles, local newsman Chick Felton was covering a murder. Having verified that the victim was dead, he sprinted to the deceased's address to ask if he could rent the now vacant apartment. The landlady shook her head: 'I already rented it to that police sergeant over there.'

OCCUPIED EUROPE:
UNDER THE SWASTIKA

A Frenchman weeps as the flags of fallen France are marched

through Marseilles, en route for Africa. Numbed by the shock of defeat,

fearful of enemy reprisals, ordinary people in occupied Europe were powerless to

halt the Nazi war machine. Some collaborated with the enemy.

A handful began resistance. But the great majority

simply continued to survive as best they could. Life had to go on . . .

THE SHADOW FALLS

The pale, grey-green uniforms of German soldiers in the streets ...

the road blocks and checking of papers ... the background menace of the Gestapo ...

all were features of occupation life.

BETWEEN APRIL and June 1940, the Germans overran six western European nations: Denmark, Norway, Luxembourg, Holland, Belgium and France. And wherever their armies struck, the frightened and bewildered masses were left not only homeless but leaderless.

Widespread bombing of airfields, the destruction of communications and military strong points, and the storming of bridges and railway stations all contributed to the Nazi *Blitzkrieg,* or lightning war. The millions who were sent scurrying out of their path found no completely safe refuge. German dive bombers tore out of the sky to rake the crowded roads and railway lines with gunfire. And by the time the stunned citizens started to drift back to the cities they found them already transformed.

In Paris, which fell on June 14, the swastika flew from the Eiffel Tower and the Arc de Triomphe. While German tanks loomed at strategic positions such as bridges and squares, German vehicles moved along the boulevards proclaiming by loudspeaker that curfew began at 8pm. Signs appeared over certain cinemas, restaurants and even brothels, reserving them for the use of German soldiers. Posters went up on the walls demanding that all orders of the military governor must be obeyed, while reassuring people that as long as they offered no resistance their safety and property would be respected.

Demoralised by the collapse of their own army, Parisians could only watch in grim silence as German units paraded down the Champs Elysées. Every day under the occupation, a changing of the Nazi guard was to be staged there at noon, complete with goose-stepping columns and military music.

OCCUPATION
Germans parade through the heart of
Paris on the day of its fall, June 14, 1940.

HOMEWARD BOUND Parisian
refugees return to the French
capital with toddler and grand-
mother bundled into prams.

'I USED TO IMAGINE THE GESTAPO WERE ROUND EVERY CORNER'

COPENHAGEN, 1943

❝ I was scared nearly all the time, I think everyone was. The thought of being arrested and tortured was very, very frightening. It was the little things that got to you, like meeting a friend in a restaurant and becoming aware that someone sitting nearby seemed interested in our conversation. Walking the streets at night, when it was very silent, very dark, I used to imagine the Gestapo were round every corner waiting for me. I kept on the move all the time and never stayed in the same place for more than a couple of nights.

The worst moments were at night, trying to get to sleep. Every time I heard a car in the street, I would jump out of bed to see if the Gestapo were outside. But I never considered giving up; once you are in something like that, you just cannot walk away. ❞

From the recollections of Christian Algreen-Petersen, a Danish Resistance worker.

By the terms of the armistice, France was divided. Though the Germans occupied the northern area they allowed the southern half of the country to be ruled by a sympathetic French Government based at the small spa town of Vichy. The aged Marshal Philippe Pétain, hero of World War I, headed the autocratic regime. The Germans were to occupy Vichy France in 1942, but for the time being Pétain was able to present himself as the man who 'saved' France. And indeed, most ordinary French families felt relief that the armistice had spared the country massive bloodshed.

Throughout Western Europe, millions were to take a similarly pragmatic view. Life had to go on, and armed resistance seemed futile in the early days of the German triumph. Though the Germans ruled either through military governors or through civilian commanders, they also made use where possible of cooperative politicians, mayors and police chiefs.

In the reopened cafés of Paris, German soldiers drank at tables elbow to elbow with Frenchmen. The Opéra and the Comédie Française played to stalls packed with officers in full dress uniform, while Maurice Chevalier sang as usual at the Casino de Paris. Horses started racing again at Auteuil in October 1940. Hermann Goering entertained his friends lavishly at Maxim's restaurant while ordinary citizens started contenting themselves with swedes and Jerusalem artichokes.

NEW ORDER IN EUROPE

From the outset, there were right-wing groups in Europe who welcomed the Germans with open arms. On April 9, 1940, when the Germans seized Norway, the country's National Socialist leader Vidkun Quisling seized power, declaring himself prime minister. Though opposition from various influential people caused the Germans to remove him temporarily, he was back 18 months later as premier,

HASTY DEPARTURE British troops halt by the wayside while Belgian refugees stream past.

heading a collaborationist government. To this day the word 'quisling' has survived in the English language as the term for a traitor serving as puppet leader for an enemy occupying his country.

The Dutch and the Danes, too, had home-grown Nazi movements, whilst Belgium had a flourishing fascist party called the Rexists. To help foster the idea of an authoritarian New Order in Europe, the Germans founded groups modelled on the Hitler Youth in each of the occupied countries. Posters appeared on walls inviting young men to volunteer for foreign divisions of the Waffen SS. Some 50,000 men from the occupied countries would accept the offer and fight for Hitler during the war.

Coexisting with the occupiers was a difficult business; shadowy liaisons were formed and the boundary between reluctant cooperation and eager collaboration was not always easy to delineate. Girls who went out with German soldiers tended to form a despised class – in Denmark they were known as 'field mattresses'.

But millions worked in the German war factories, and all sorts of 'understandings' were arrived at. There were restaurateurs and bar owners who, through being agreeable to their German clients, might put a word in the right ear to secure the release of a prisoner. Highly placed German officers and officials had influence to dispense, and their favours could mean life or death to a Jewish family, for

SOLO JOURNEY

In occupied Paris patriots sabotaged the forced-labour programme. A train was scheduled to leave the Gare de l'Est in October 1942 with 400 workers bound for Germany. Only 27 men turned up at the station. Speeches were made none the less and a brass band played to give them a send-off. As the engine chugged slowly away from the platform, however, loud laughter burst from the crowd. The carriages did not move – someone had uncoupled them – and the locomotive puffed bravely off alone.

example, or a draft evader, or a resistance worker.

Despite all the pressures to cooperate with the occupiers, a certain spirit of passive resistance was present from the earliest days. Sometimes, for example, a patriot would pointedly get up and leave a shop or café as soon as a German entered. In Parisian cinemas, the Germans were forced to ban applause because people would clap and cheer at inappropriate moments. In Dutch cinemas people walked out so often when German propaganda films began that a law was passed banning such early departures.

Patriotic graffiti appeared overnight on German wall posters. In Denmark, girls took to wearing knitted caps bearing the bull's-eye emblem of

ROAD BLOCK French motorists have their papers checked by the occupiers, 1940.

SEARCHING QUESTIONS Germans investigate a lorry stopped at the border between occupied and Vichy France.

Britain's Royal Air Force, and the elderly King Christian X became for his people a focus of dignified defiance.

Strike action was taken in many countries against particularly unpopular measures. In Norway, for example, Quisling tried to get history taught from a Nazi standpoint, but every history teacher in the country rejected the new syllabus, and all were arrested. Then Quisling tried to get all teachers to join a political union: 12,000 out of 14,000 resigned rather than do so. The schools were closed, and only reopened when Quisling backed down.

Defiance also took the form of tuning in to British radio broadcasts. With Nazi censorship of the Press and radio, access to an alternative source of information was vital to any patriot's morale. By the spring of 1942 the BBC was broadcasting in 24 different languages. It was over the BBC on June 18, 1940, that a young French general called Charles de

HATS OFF Caps in RAF colours, worn in Denmark to indicate Allied sympathies, were banned in 1943.

Gaulle called on his defeated countrymen to continue the struggle. 'Whatever happens,' he declared, 'the flame of French resistance must not be quenched and will not be quenched.'

As the war went on and resistance increased, the BBC was able to give further assistance to patriots in the occupied territories. Every night on the foreign programme scores of 'personal messages' were broadcast: 'Romeo kisses Juliet', 'Barbara's dog will have three puppies', and so on. These puzzling utterances were coded messages to particular resistance movements announcing, for example, the safe arrival of a courier or the impending arrival of three fugitives on an escape line.

FATHER FIGURE Marshal Pétain asks for aid for war-stricken families.

SECOURS NATIONAL

ILS ONT FROID
ILS ONT FAIM

Aidez-moi

A LES SECOURIR

NEW DIRECTIONS German street signs on a Paris avenue point to key sites for occupation troops.

WARTIME FASHION

Shortages and rationing imposed severe restrictions on the
fashion industry, but designers refused to be defeated.

SHORT SKIRTS AND SENSIBLE, flat-heeled shoes . . . square-shouldered jackets that recalled the cut of uniforms . . . these were basic features of the wartime 'Utility Look' for women

FASHIONABLE OCCUPATION
Paris designers produced simple but stylish fashions, such as this Cristobal Balenciaga dress of 1943. Right: Military overtones were fashionable in Germany.

everywhere. World War II had a profound impact on fashion, even in Paris, the international centre of *haute couture*.

Soon after the occupation, the Nazis ordered the entire Paris fashion industry to move to Berlin, and although they eventually withdrew the order several couture houses closed down. Vionnet retired and Schiaparelli went into exile. 'Coco' Chanel had shut up shop a year before the outbreak of war and was to earn opprobrium under the occupation by taking a top Nazi official as her lover. Expensive types of silk and lace were no longer available in the

French capital, and humbler fabrics were restricted. The Paris clothing trade was also diminished by the fact that a lot of its workers were of Jewish origin and forced to flee abroad – or to Vichy France (many settled in the area around Nice and Marseilles).

However, a few fashion houses continued to produce some new designs, catering chiefly for wealthy collaborators, or exporting their creations to Germany. As if in defiance of wartime constraints, they brought out fanciful creations with platform shoes, elaborately draped bodices, skirts that were fuller than those seen elsewhere, and sometimes even fur coats. For some people, all such luxuries smacked of collaboration – or black market connections – and when Paris was liberated in 1944, Allied observers expressed shock at the flamboyance on view. 'It seems terrible to see huge velvet skirts and sequins when the world is at war', a WAC commented. The designers argued, however, that flouting clothing restrictions was an act of defiance against the Germans.

While Americans and Britons knew that by saving cloth they were assisting the Allied cause, the French designers claimed that the more material they used the less was available to the enemy.

In Paris, one particular extravagance was the fancifully trimmed hat or turban. Some milliners produced examples that tilted precariously forward or burst from the wearer's head

HAT APPEAL
In France clothes were rationed, but nothing prevented a woman from sporting an eccentric hat.

in a tall explosion of fabric. They were copied by many French women, for flowers and feathers were not rationed and the hat was one place where the wearer could make a splash with a minimum of material. Women even used wood shavings for decoration.

In Britain, silk stockings were in very short supply by December 1940. To take their place, various brands of leg make-up appeared, and women resorted to drawing in seams with an eyebrow pencil down the back of each leg.

BLACKOUT BAG This stylish fashion accessory came with a flashlight and emergency kit.

THE AUSTERITY LOOK
American fashions came of age, combining stylishness and practicality. English designers created the austerity look (right) to conserve resources. French designers, meanwhile, continued to cater for a sophisticated and elegant clientele (below).

A general blackout on news from occupied Europe meant that fashion followers in Britain and the United States could no longer seek inspiration from Paris. One result was to liberate some American designers, who now had greater freedom to develop their own styles. Since the United States was less troubled by rationing, the American woman with her fuller skirts, nylon stockings and high-heeled shoes in bright leather became the envy of Europe. New York, it was predicted, would become the fashion capital of the world. And although the claim was exaggerated,

the Americans did begin to set the style in the areas of work and leisure wear.

The designer Claire McCardell, producing clothes for the career woman, is usually regarded as the great pioneer of the comfortable 'American look'. Her clothes, she said, stood for 'freedom, democracy, and casualness'.

In due course, Levi jeans and the Sloppy Joe sweaters worn by many American teenagers would sweep the youth of the Western World. Even in wartime, the United States proved capable of teenage trend-setting. On the streets of occupied Paris, youngsters learned of the zoot suit craze sweeping America and they created their own 'zazou' look based upon it, consisting of drape jackets and thick-soled shoes. The zazou were flashy and delinquent, and they took to swing music as a later generation would take to rock 'n' roll.

SLOGANS IN SILK
Scarves were printed with defence slogans and the sayings of the British premier Winston Churchill.

STEPPING OUT
Although sensible, flat-heeled shoes were the basic style of wartime, women still yearned for more elegant, high-heeled designs.

RATIONING AND DEPRIVATION

The occupied peoples endured a drab existence. 'Finally,' wrote the French philosopher

Jean-Paul Sartre, 'we spoke of nothing but food – the hunt for food bargains

was the only enterprise still within our scope.'

PERFORMING IN PARIS under the occupation, Maurice Chevalier popularised a song called *Symphonie des Semelles de Bois* (Symphony of the Wooden Soles). Because shoe leather was in desperately short supply, 24 million pairs of wooden-soled shoes were turned out annually by French manufacturers, and their clattering on the pavements was for many the authentic sound of the occupation.

Shortages affected life in countless ways. With petrol needed for German use, private cars virtually disappeared from the roads of occupied Europe. In Paris, motor cabs were replaced by fleets of *vélo* taxis (bicycle taxis) with sidecars attached or cabs pulled behind the cyclist. Charcoal-burning vehicles, known in France as *gazogènes,* were introduced: slow to start and erratic to drive, they needed replenishing with new charcoal every 30 miles (50km) or so.

Rationing was introduced in the occupied countries not long after the Germans took over. Administering the system was a huge task for bureaucrats, worsened by the fact that, as the war progressed, local clerks had to look out increasingly for irregularities in people's ration cards. The black market did a lively trade in restricted goods, and the resistance took to forging stamps and stealing ration books to feed the growing numbers of men hiding to avoid the forced-labour draft.

EATING TULIPS

During the 'hunger winter' of 1944–45 the Dutch were reduced to eating their famous tulips. The bulbs were roasted on stoves, and proved palatable, though prone to give people indigestion.

MEAL TICKETS
To buy sandwiches, the French needed tickets which were cut from coupon sheets (above).

WARTIME TAXIS To combat petrol shortages, bicycle cabs appeared on the Paris streets. Another innovation was the electric taxi (right).

Queues outside the shops grew ever longer, and numbered slips were often issued to those waiting in line so that they could keep their place. In Paris, people sometimes camped overnight on makeshift beds outside butchers' shops. The butchers tried to discourage the practice by refusing to acknowledge any queue that formed more than 30 minutes before opening. In response, the queues were formed round the corner, out of sight, and appeared fully organised at the appropriate time.

Throughout Europe, queues also formed, especially outside tobacconists. People waited for a daily ration that often failed to materialise, the allowance being exhausted before a shopper reached the counter. Before long, people were drying and pulverising everything from nettle leaves and lime flowers to Jerusalem artichokes. In Amsterdam they tried smoking a tea substitute – made chiefly from dried strawberry leaves – in their pipes.

New foods entered the diet: soya beans, peanut flour and casein (a tasteless white protein made from milk). The cities suffered from hunger more than the country, for although rural areas were plundered for food, country folk were better equipped than town dwellers to cope with hardships. They had reasonable access to firewood, for example, and there were age-old peasant traditions of self-sufficiency and of concealing produce from the tax gatherer.

As a result, many townsfolk made weekly train or bicycle trips to the country, coming back with baskets laden with what food they could obtain. As coal, gas and electricity were increasingly restricted, the time came when families had barely enough fuel to cook their evening meals. Those lucky enough to have friends in the country did their cooking on wood stoves out of town, where faggots were still plentiful. On good days they returned to their grateful friends and relatives bearing such luxuries as cold chicken, hard-boiled eggs and salt pork – perhaps a pâté of rabbit meat, too.

Wartime train journeys with their crowded corridors and compartments, and the annoyance of inspectors' spot checks, were among many housewives' most vivid memories of the occupation days. Everything was drab and malodorous. Drue Tartière, making regular trips between Melun and Paris, recalled: 'Since there was a great shortage of soap, the smells in the train were almost overpowering. It was chic to be shabby in France at this time, for only collaborators could afford to dress well.'

Personal hygiene was not helped by the fact that the only soap officially available came in hard grey cakes that were said to rot the clothes they were supposed to wash. In the Paris Métro stations, which unwashed masses used for air-raid shelters, the stench defied belief.

And the cold winters were almost unendurable. With the German authorities seizing coal supplies for the war effort, many people took to going to bed straight after the meagre evening meal.

Even wealthy women, accustomed to sheer silks and lisles, took to wearing thick woollen stockings and hand-knitted gloves. People scrounged and scavenged and made do, shaping blouses from bedsheets and dresses from curtain material. Men packed old newspapers under their threadbare suits. In Paris, the celebrated writer Colette sat in her apartment in the Palais Royal staring at empty fireplaces and wondering whether certain pieces of furniture might not be worth more to her as firewood.

In some European cities, conditions reached crisis point. Athens, for example, was stricken by a terrible hunger as a result of a British blockade combined with German neglect during the winter of 1941–42. Many people died of starvation there before Red Cross famine workers helped to relieve the situation. And cities in Holland were to suffer appallingly during the winter of 1944–45.

The Dutch government in exile had called for a railway strike, and in reprisal the German authorities refused to transport food or fuel to cities in the Amsterdam region. Motor vehicles had been confiscated, and the river barges were very largely in the hands of the

THE BLACK MARKET

WHEREVER shortages occurred in occupied Europe, shifty figures could be found with access to supplies. Food and tobacco were the mainstay of the black market, and its scope was enormous: wines from the Mediterranean travelled to northern Europe, for instance, while potatoes travelled south. The Gestapo infiltrated many black-market operations, however, partly to keep tabs on their connections with the Resistance, and partly to supplement their own pay from this lucrative trade.

ILLICIT SNACK Sandwiches sold by an Italian black marketeer.

Wehrmacht. The food ration dwindled to a weekly 3lb (1.3kg) of bread, 4lb (1.8kg) of potatoes and a little cheese. No meat, fat, eggs, sugar or milk were available. By October, emergency soup kitchens were doling out vegetable stews to 160,000 people per day in Amsterdam alone.

HOLLAND'S HUNGER WINTER

Pulped sugar beet – normally fed only to pigs – was served at dinner tables. People even ate tulip bulbs. Domestic cats vanished, reappearing in butchers' shops where they were presented as 'roof rabbit'. Bakers' carts had to be protected by police for fear of looters. Barbers trimmed their clients in return for potatoes; the wealthy bartered fur coats for food.

Meanwhile, shivering citizens felled trees in the parks for firewood. Homes in the now-derelict Jewish quarter were gutted for floorboards and beams. Mobs even braved German troops to raid evacuated houses in the prohibited coastal zone. As the crisis deepened in Holland, the sanitation system broke down. Sewage spilled onto the streets, lingering in noxious pools.

Rats multiplied too, and were sometimes seen nibbling at the corpses assembled in the churches;

GROW YOUR OWN   A Dutch poster promotes vegetable gardening. Left: beans are cultivated in the gardens of the Louvre, Paris.

PARIS, 1940 Swastikas emblazon this Paris restaurant, reserved for German soldiers. It was conveniently situated opposite the Moulin Rouge – a nightclub much frequented by the occupiers.

PAPERS, PERMITS AND PASSES

AN EXTRAORDINARY number of personal papers was needed by people living under the occupation, and had to be carried by just about any adult stepping outside his or her own front door. The array included:

1. An identity card giving the citizen's name, parentage, birth date, place of birth and marital state.

2. A work permit with qualifications and place of employment.

3. A ration card.

4. A tobacco card (whether the holder smoked or not).

5. If near a coast or frontier, a permit to be in the relevant zone.

6. If male, demobilisation papers identifying the unit from which the man had been discharged.

7. If male, a medical certificate signed by an identifiable doctor, stating what health reasons exempted the holder from immediate deportation for forced labour in Germany (necessary after midsummer 1942).

Add such necessities as a driving licence and an insurance certificate for any vehicle, and the total amounted to a hefty walletful of documents which any police authority might order a citizen to produce at a spot check.

---

bodies sometimes remained unburied for days because the timber shortage had left coffins in short supply. The scenes in Dutch cities came to resemble the morbid images depicted in medieval pictures of the Dance of Death, and to escape the horror thousands started trekking out into the countryside.

They headed north, especially, for the farming provinces of Friesland and Groningen, carrying with them bundled linen, china, jewellery and gold rings in hopes of bartering them for peas, bacon or beans. Many dropped along the road, and those who did reach the rich farmlands often found people unwilling to do business with them. Signs reading 'No bartering' were erected by farmers to discourage the ragged armies of frozen, hollow-eyed city dwellers who arrived at their gates.

By the beginning of 1945, the official food ration had dropped to 500 calories per day – even less than in the German concentration camps. Altogether some 16,000 Dutch men, women and children starved to death or perished of cold in the appalling 'hunger winter' of 1944–45.

FIGHTING HUNGER **Rations distributed by the Allies after the famine that struck Holland during the winter of 1944–45. Right: a Dutch poster from the same time suggests collecting acorns for food.**

THE JEWISH AGONY

Deportation to the camps was the fate awaiting Jewish families throughout occupied Europe.

Those who managed to slip the Nazis' vast net lived in the utmost secrecy and fear

of betrayal and arrest.

WE ARE GOING to destroy the Jews', Hitler told the Czech foreign minister in January 1939, and those who doubted his intention to do so at the outset of the occupation were to be terribly disabused. But the persecution often came in stages.

In Paris, for example, a census of Jews was ordered first and all Jewish-owned businesses were required to display signs proclaiming them to be so, in black letters on a yellow background. Jews were required to wear the yellow six-pointed star of David on their outer clothing. Restaurants, cafés, cinemas and theatres were declared out of bounds to them – as were public telephone booths.

Later, on July 16, 1942, came the Parisians' ultimate shame. A police trawl of the capital netted some 13,000 Jewish men, women and children. They were assembled in a sports stadium, the Vélodrome d'Hiver, where they were ordered to wait with their bundled possessions for trains to Germany – and the concentration camps.

Throughout occupied Europe a similar pattern of events occurred, provoking a lot of ill-feeling among non-Jews. Indeed, some even took to wearing yellow stars of their own, marked in the middle with (instead of 'Jew') 'Roman Catholic', 'Protestant', or even 'Buddhist' or 'Zulu'.

Denmark had a Jewish population of about 8000. The Germans ordered their round-up to begin at 10pm on Friday October 1, 1943, the start of the Jewish New Year. News reached the intended victims in advance, however, and by nightfall most had vanished into the homes of non-Jewish friends and acquaintances. Only 284 Jews were caught in the German net that night.

More than half of Norway's Jewish population slipped across the border into Sweden before deportations began. In Belgium, the Dowager Queen Elisabeth was able to save thousands from

---

'A SONG-BIRD WHOSE WINGS HAVE BEEN BRUTALLY CLIPPED'

AMSTERDAM, OCTOBER 29, 1943

❝ My nerves often get the better of me: it is especially on Sundays that I feel rotten. The atmosphere is so oppressive, and sleepy and heavy as lead. You don't hear a single bird singing outside, and a deadly close silence hangs everywhere, catching hold of me as if it will drag me down deep into an underworld.

At such times Daddy, Mummy and Margot leave me cold. I wander from one room to another, downstairs and up again, feeling like a song-bird whose wings have been brutally clipped and who is beating itself in

utter darkness against the bars of its cage. "Go outside, laugh, and take a breath of fresh air," a voice cries within me, but I don't even feel a response any more; I go and lie on the divan and sleep, to make the time pass more quickly, and the stillness and the terrible fear, because there is no way of killing them. ❞

From the diary of Anne Frank.

DAILY TERROR Even the vivacious Anne Frank succumbed to terror while in hiding.

REPRESSION French police supervise a round-up of Jews in Paris, 1941. Right: wearing the star of David, French Jews work in an open-air laundry.

PERSECUTION CONTINUES The propaganda poster claims that de Gaulle is a tool of international Jewry. Above: a raid on Jews in Amsterdam.

deportation by interceding with the German authorities. In Holland, Jewish families had for centuries been especially prominent in the nation's cultural life, and there was widespread opposition to the Nazis' racial policies. Moves against Jewish professors provoked strikes among non-Jewish students at the universities of Leiden and Delft, which were shut down as a result. In February 1941, when local Nazis beat up some 400 Jews at random and had them sent to Mauthausen – which was already known to be a death camp – there was a general strike in Amsterdam which eventually spread to nearby towns.

Piet Nak, a Communist street cleaner, was among those who stood up in public and urged people to down tools. 'We were filled with an overwhelming hate. We'd never seen anything like that in Amsterdam: lots of people, just because they were Jewish ... just arrested and beaten up.'

Despite protests like these, however, the methodical registration and segregation of Jewish families continued in Holland. And as the Germans stepped up their policy of deportation, dragging people from their houses by night, shoving them into vans and carting them off to railway stations, more and more Jews went into hiding. They were concealed in attics, cellars, farmers' barns and so on.

The Jewish schoolgirl Anne Frank was 13 when she went into hiding in 1942 with her parents and sister and four other people. For two years they were kept safe in the sealed-off back rooms of an Amsterdam office building, aided by her father's non-Jewish employees. In her diary, Anne wrote all about the tensions in their little community, the problems of growing up, her moments of despair and her unswerving faith. But in August 1944 the family was betrayed. Armed German security police, accompanied by Dutch Nazis, burst into their 'secret annexe' and all were arrested. Anne Frank was to die of typhoid at the concentration camp at Belsen early in March 1945.

SPORT IN WARTIME

Despite the loss of leading players to the services, many sports survived the privations of the war – and even flourished.

SPORT was an inevitable casualty of the war. The Olympic Games scheduled for 1940 and 1944 were cancelled, for example, as were the soccer World Cup competitions for 1942 and 1946. All over the world top sporting personalities were called up for military service.

In Britain, many sports grounds were closed, bombed or requisitioned for war use. Wimbledon, for example, was hit by a German bomb which flattened a corner of the Centre Court on October 11, 1940.

Association football remained Britain's favourite game but when the season started in 1939 the leagues had to be reorganised on a regional basis because of the limitations of wartime transport. Arsenal, the top English club, lost all but two of its 44 professionals to the services and like other teams had to make up numbers with a mixture of professionals stationed locally, part-timers who lived in the neighbourhood, youngsters and volunteers.

Sporting events drew huge crowds on the American home front, despite the loss of many leading players to the services. In baseball the highest-paid major leaguer was Hank Greenberg (earning $55,000 a year) and he was in uniform within a month of Pearl Harbor, along with ace pitcher Bob Feller of the Cleveland Indians. The New York Yankees' great Joe DiMaggio continued to delight crowds all through the 1942 season but was drafted the following year.

Fans flocked to football games in the United States, especially college games, and boxing flourished too. Defending his heavyweight crown in January 1942 at Madison Square Garden, the 'Brown Bomber' Joe Louis decked his opponent, Buddy Baer, in the first round. Louis won patriotic approval through donating his share of the winnings to the Navy Relief Fund. Three days later the boxer was drafted into the army.

Sports had a huge importance in the Axis countries, which gloried in physical fitness and celebrated it at countless games and displays. In Italy, Mussolini described boxing as a typically Fascist form of self-expression.

In Nazi Germany, the *Kraft durch Freude* (Strength through Joy) movement promoted healthy outdoor activities. The Berlin Olympics of 1936 had been conceived as a dazzling demonstration of the supremacy of Nordic athletes; the Games had been marred for the Nazis by the fact that the star athlete turned out to be Jesse Owens, a black American, who beat the cream of German youth to win four gold medals. But racist myths were perpetuated at various games held in occupied Europe, from which non-

BIG HITTER
Baseball's Joe DiMaggio was among America's great wartime sporting heroes.
Right: college football was affected from 1942, when the draft was extended to 18–19 year olds, but it kept going through the war years.

THE SATURDAY EVENING POST

BEGINNING A FOOTBALL SERIAL

UNDER THE BOMBS An aircraft spotter at a British football match.
Right: cricketers at Lord's cricket ground duck as a doodle-bug flies by
during a match between the Army and the RAF, July 1944.

Aryans were excluded, and Hitler still nourished his dreams for a Germanic New Order. Among other tasks, Albert Speer was asked to prepare plans for a gigantic new German stadium capable of holding 400,000 people. All Olympic Games were to be staged there, 'for all time to come'. The dream died, however, as Germany met increasing setbacks in the war. Early in 1943, as part of the new commitment to 'Total War', the Nazi authorities ordered press reports on sporting events to be curtailed – and professional sport in Germany stopped altogether.

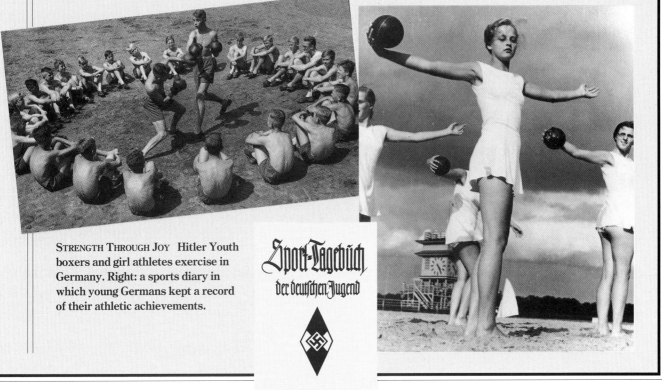

STRENGTH THROUGH JOY Hitler Youth boxers and girl athletes exercise in Germany. Right: a sports diary in which young Germans kept a record of their athletic achievements.

Sport-Tagebuch
der deutschen Jugend

LEISTUNGSSTEIGERUNG DURCH LEISTUNGSPRÜFUNG

WORKING FOR THE REICH

The Nazis trawled Europe for manpower just as they stripped it of food and fuel.

However, no other action in the history of occupied Europe provoked such widespread

hostility as the forced-labour programme.

WITH DESPERATE labour shortages in German farms and factories, the occupiers put a big propaganda effort into recruiting volunteers from the conquered nations to do work in the Fatherland. 'Through working in Germany,' read one French poster, 'you will be an ambassador for French quality.' Another, depicting an heroic German soldier, read: 'They gave their blood – give your work to save Europe from Bolshevism.'

Recruiting offices were opened in both zones of France, and in June 1942 Hitler's manpower director, Gauleiter Fritz Sauckel, came to the country in person to demand 350,000 workers from the collaborationist leader Pierre Laval. Attempting to delay the imposition of forced labour, Laval introduced a scheme called *la relève* (the relief) by which one French prisoner of war would be repatriated for every three workers who left the country.

By the end of August, however, only 50,000 Frenchmen had answered the call, and they did not find working conditions in Germany as appealing as the posters had led them to believe. Herded together in barracks, they worked 12 hours a day for wages that were heavily taxed.

To counter the disappointing response, the Germans made louder threats to use compulsion. The Vichy Government now required all medically fit Frenchmen of military age, and all single women aged 21–35, to be available for work that was judged beneficial to the nation. It was an unpopular move, which provoked strikes and demonstrations.

But still the German thirst for workers remained unquenched, and in the end forced labour was inflicted on the population in the form of *Service du Travail Obligatoire* (compulsory work service). There were 600,000 French conscripts by 1944 – and about a third of them ended up working in concentration camps.

THE NEW EXPLOSIVE

Plastic explosive, a new material available from June 1940, was the saboteur's friend, coming in malleable blocks that could be stuck to a bridge or railway line with adhesive tape. It was also safe to handle, since it needed a detonator to explode it. One agent in the Pyrenees even used it as fuel on his cottage fire because of the coal shortage. It terrified his colleagues – but burned safely.

EXPLOSIVE DEVICE *Maquis* **members sabotage a railway line in France, 1944.**

LABOUR FRONT 'I work in Germany', proclaims this poster, inviting other Frenchmen to do their bit for the Reich.

Text on image: IGLAIS ASSASSINS. MORT aux JUIFS / LES ZAZOUS A LA RELEVE / FRANCE-EUROP / HEIL HITLER!

Text on poster: TOI AUSSI! / TES CAMARADES T'ATTENDENT / DANS LA DIVISION FRANÇAISE DE LA / WAFFEN-SS

SEND OFF French volunteers leave Paris in 1943 to join the Waffen SS, the military wing of Hitler's security force. Nearly 50,000 men from occupied Europe fought for the Nazis. Top: the poster calls for more SS recruits.

Tapping France for its labour reserve may have helped the Reich in the short term, but the scheme also rebounded on the Germans, for tens of thousands of young Frenchmen went into hiding to avoid the compulsory work service. Seeking refuge in wild country, the evaders formed ragged bands that came to be known as *maquis,* a Corsican word meaning bushy scrubland and referring to the mountain thickets where that island's outlaws had long held

sway. Supplied by Allied airdrops, and aided by secret agents and officers of the disbanded French armed forces, the fugitives were to form scattered armies of resistance fighters.

The draft also had a more general psychological effect on ordinary French families. People were shocked by the sudden round-ups of able-bodied men, and the trawls through factories and villages. Those who had watched with indifference as Jews or isolated resisters succumbed to the Nazi terror now felt more closely bonded to the Resistance.

The same was true wherever the Germans introduced forced labour. The policy soured relations between the occupying troops and the civilian

TOIL AND TROUBLE Propaganda posters and German employment bureaus appeared abroad. But people, like the Frenchwoman above, who went to work in Germany found conditions hard.

populations and made for some dramatic face-to-face confrontations.

In November 1944, as Holland was swept for men to do labour service, Mrs J.F. Bubberman-Boer recalled: 'When the doorbell rang there were two Germans. Both came upstairs. One stayed at the top of the stairs and the other came into the room. He looked around the room and the two men who were there had to get dressed and go with them.

'We being women were crying, of course, both of us, one woman with a baby in her arms and another hanging on her skirts. And I can still remember vividly the one German who was inside the room. He was crying – tears were streaming down his face and he said: "I am so terribly sorry, but I'm not alone. I'd love to be able to help you but I can't do anything because there's someone with me and I don't know him." He couldn't do it – he'd have tried very hard to leave those two men there because he thought it was terrible. That was the first time I'd ever seen a German cry. He really cried – big tears rolling down his face.'

'NOW YOU'LL SEE HOW WE DO IT'

PARIS, 1944

❝ It was getting particularly unhealthy for the enemy to walk through the streets of Paris ... One day when I was hurrying along a bridge across the Seine ... two young Frenchmen walked quickly past me. They were following a Nazi officer in front of them. As they passed me, they said something to me which sounded like, "Now you'll see how we do it". Before I knew what was happening, one of them had stuck a knife between the shoulder blades of the Nazi officer, and before the Nazi could hit the pavement, the other had him by the seat of his pants and had hurled him into the Seine. I and the other spectators on the bridge that afternoon ran as fast as we could to get out of the neighbourhood, not even daring to look back. ❞

From the recollections of Drue Tartière, an American-born Parisian.

RESISTANCE AND REPRESSION

Blowing up railways, forging papers, hiding Allied agents, working underground presses –

these were just a few of the tasks undertaken by the ordinary men and women

of the European resistance in the fight against Fascism.

ON FRIDAY, MAY 8, 1942, a nondescript little French house painter named René Duchez arrived at the offices of the Organisation Todt at Caen in Normandy. The organisation was charged with building Hitler's Atlantic Wall, a colossal system of defences against the threatened Allied invasion: blockhouses, minefields and gun emplacements were to stretch along the whole west coast of Europe, from Norway to the Pyrenees.

Duchez found himself momentarily alone. There was a pile of maps on a desk, and with an odd sense of hysteria he realised he was looking at a top-secret chart of the Normandy coastline. Impulsively, Duchez took the map and slipped it behind a gilt-framed mirror on the wall. Five days later, when he had finished decorating the room, he was able to retrieve the map and smuggle it out of the building in the bottom of an old paint tin.

When unfolded, Duchez's stolen map turned out to be over two yards long, an extraordinarily detailed blueprint of a key section of the Normandy defences. It showed everything from major fortifications and underground tunnels to the positions of individual flamethrowers. Passed on to the Resistance leader Gilbert Renault, the map was conveyed secretly to England on board a fishing vessel, and was to prove invaluable to the Allied chiefs of staff planning the D-Day invasions.

Ordinary people like Duchez formed the backbone of the Resistance – men, women and children, too, who were often sick with fear as they carried out their work of sabotage, gathering intelligence, aiding crashed airmen, printing and distributing underground newspapers and so on. Allied agencies such as Britain's SOE (Special Operations Executive) and the American OSS (Office of Strategic Services) sent trained agents to direct efforts, and the governments in exile also formed their own secret services working in occupied territory. But the rank and file were drawn from ordinary families on the home front: house painters, shop girls, farm boys, railwaymen, doctors, housewives, trawlermen.

They knew the risks they were running. But as the war dragged on and a German victory looked increasingly less certain, more and more civilians were prepared to take chances. The introduction of forced labour, in particular, swelled the ranks of the secret armies, and as the Nazi repression deepened, ever more people came to loathe the sound of jackboots on the cobblestones, the sight of street round-ups and the manhandling of deportees into trucks. Every once in a while the surface normality of life under the occupation was shattered by a moment of stark horror – like the time when a young Parisian, fleeing the nightmare of Gestapo interrogation, slashed his wrists to die slowly and

CAUGHT IN THE ACT Penalties for sabotage were severe throughout occupied Europe.

FALLEN LEAF
In 1941, the Allies dropped leaf-shaped leaflets in enemy territory to rebut German promises of victory. Propaganda played a major role in the struggle against Nazism.

Die Blätter fallen
Münchner Neueste Nachrichten
1941 wird das Jahr des Endsieges werden
Der versprochene Endsieg bleibt aus

in public on the pavement of the Rue des Jacobins.

Various German bodies were employed to break the Resistance, from the notorious Gestapo (state police) and SD (security service), which were both Nazi organisations, to the Abwehr, Germany's regular army security and intelligence organisation. Collaborationist bodies were formed too, earning the peculiar hatred of their countrymen because they were traitors and in some ways posed a more dangerous threat than the Germans, since they knew the resisters' language and home territory.

In France, the right-wing *Milice* (Militia) headed by Joseph Darnand was especially loathed. Its 45,000 members included many gangsters and criminals who had been recruited when French courts allowed convicted felons the choice of joining the *Milice* as an alternative to prison. Interrogation at the hands of the Gestapo and other bodies might include beatings with truncheons, electric shock treatment or the dislocation of limbs. Water torture was often used too, victims being half drowned in baths of icy water to make them talk.

To dissuade people from attacking troops, the Germans also operated a ruthless system of reprisals. In October 1941, for example, 48 people were shot at Chateaubriant in revenge for one assassinated German colonel. Alarm was such that the next day de Gaulle formally repudiated the policy of assassination over the BBC, for though reprisals on this scale certainly sharpened people's hatred for the occupiers, they also spread fear and dismay. In general the Allies damped down attempts at premature revolt, preferring instead a patient policy of training, equipping and coordinating secret armies that should be ready to act behind German lines when the D-Day landings came.

THE SECRET WAR

Arms and explosives were dropped and secret agents ferried to and from occupied Europe by black-painted Lysander aircraft making moonlight landings on remote fields. Local resisters were required to lay out an L-shaped arrangement of landing lights, and operations like these required the cooperation of many people. Once, half a French village and a team of carthorses were needed to pull a Hudson aircraft free from muddy ground.

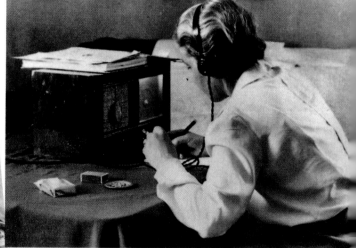

Contact with the home base in Britain was vital, and a trained radio operator, transmitting in Morse code from a suitcase-sized set, was a key need in any group.

THE SECRET WAR The tiny Dutch radio receiver (top) is hidden in a tobacco tin. Left: a Dutch resister forges papers. Above: A resistance member illegally listening to a BBC broadcast in Norway.

AN EPIDEMIC OF V SIGNS

THE V SIGN, symbolising Victory, was devised as an emblem of the Resistance by two Belgians working for the BBC Belgian Service. From January 1941 the BBC started urging listeners in Belgium to go out under cover of darkness and chalk the V sign on doors, walls and pavements. The campaign soon spread to other European countries.

The V proved to be brilliantly adaptable. The sign could be made with the fingers raised in the familiar Churchillian gesture, or tapped out in its Morse form (three dots and one dash) on a teacup, say, under the noses of the occupiers.

Haunted by the V campaign, the Germans eventually responded by attempting to appropriate the symbol for themselves. It was made to stand for *Viktoria* – an antiquated Teutonic word – and they began to print posters of their own bearing a huge white V.

EIFFEL TOWER To deflate the Allied campaign the Germans displayed the V themselves.

DEUTSCHLAND SIEGT AUF ALLEN FRONTEN

German detector vans cruised through town streets and country roads to try and get bearings on the clandestine transmitters.

In the radio war, the great aim for the Germans was to capture the operator and force him or her to send home false messages. In the celebrated Operation North Pole, Germany's Abwehr Colonel H.J. Giskes achieved precisely this, calling for ever more supplies to be sent into Holland from Britain. In 1942–43 no fewer than 52 agents and a vast tonnage of weapons and explosives were dropped in by the British SOE – only to be netted immediately on arrival.

The Resistance achieved some spectacular results of its own, however. In the 1943 Vemork raid, for example, a party of nine men attacked the Norsk Hydro plant in Norway, destroying its tanks of 'heavy water' which were needed in German experiments to make an atomic bomb. When the occupiers tried to move their last supplies of heavy water to Germany, the ferry carrying them was also destroyed – and with it all Hitler's nuclear ambitions.

SILENT ACTS OF SABOTAGE

The big bangs formed only part of the picture, however. Immeasurable damage was done to the Nazi regime in Europe by small acts of sabotage such as clerks mixing important cards in an index file; industrial workers mislaying key machine parts – or simply working at an infuriatingly slow pace.

Europe's railwaymen were past masters at making trouble like this. All goods moved under Wehrmacht orders were supposed to travel in sealed trucks, for security reasons. And by switching labels railway staff were able to send trucks for Colmar speeding to Copenhagen, trucks for Mulhouse to Nantes, and so on. On one occasion, a freightload of acid for U-boat batteries reached a steelworks in Bohemia. On another, fighter airfields awaiting supplies received

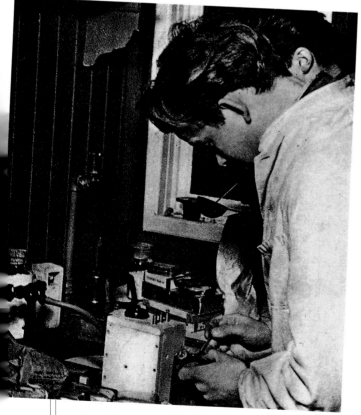

BOMB FACTORY A Danish resister makes missiles, using metal soap containers filled with explosives.

CARTOON GENIUS

Cartoonists provided newspaper and magazine readers with a light-hearted commentary on the events of the war.

'VERY WELL, ALONE' Britain fights on. Right: Churchill and Roosevelt march into Europe on the orders of Stalin, from the German paper *Kladderadatsch*.

FOR NEWSPAPER READERS in World War II, cartoonists offered a light-hearted view of a harrowing period in which lightheartedness was in short supply. Food rationing, petrol shortages, blackout drill and clothing restrictions all offered themes for humorous treatment, and even the Axis leaders were cut down to comic size. New Zealand-born David Low, lampooning Hitler and Mussolini in the *London Evening Standard*, so annoyed the top Nazis in November 1937 that Goebbels complained about his cartoons to Lord Halifax, then the Lord Privy Seal. Low's weapon was mockery. He avoided depicting the dictators as nightmarish figures, for they could then appear too powerful to resist.

Low's lasting caricatures of Hitler and Mussolini were matched by his Colonel Blimp – he was the very embodiment of Britain's own reactionary stupidity. Low also possessed an extraordinary ability to concentrate his energies on a mighty theme, providing a focus for emotional release. One of his most stirring images was published in June 1940 after the fall of Dunkirk and depicted Britain as a clifftop foot soldier, solitary and defiant, under the heading 'Very well, alone'. A similar commitment typified the work of the other great political satirists of the time. One of these was the American David Fitzpatrick, publishing in the St Louis *Post-Dispatch*. Another was the Russian Boris Efimov, who worked for *Izvestia* and was so valued by the authorities that, it was said, he was paid 6000 roubles a month – four times the official salary of Stalin.

In Germany, all cartoons that appeared in newspapers or magazines between 1939 and 1945 were subject to strict censorship laws. The cost of transgressing them was high: the cartoonist Erich Ohser, alias E.O. Plauen, well known for the strip cartoons that appeared in the *Berliner Illustrierte Zeitung* before the war, died in a Nazi prison in 1944.

For the United States, Bill Mauldin depicted the hardships of the foot-slogging infantryman or 'dogface' through his immortal GIs, Willie and Joe. The 19-year-old Mauldin enlisted in 1940 'because he had run out of pencils'

COMIC PHILOSOPHER Colonel Blimp regularly berated British readers.

COMIC-STRIP WARRIORS Sad Sack, the US army private, represented the everyday reality of war, while the tantalising Jane boosted British morale. Right: In a French publication, Churchill the bulldog is surrounded by London in ruins during the Blitz.

and pulled no punches about the conditions on the fighting front. 'This damn tree leaks', runs the caption to one of his cartoons. Another: 'I wish I could stand up and get some sleep.'

THE ASSASSIN A US view of the Japanese attack on Pearl Harbor published in the St Louis *Post-Dispatch* in December 1941.

The war gave America another immortal in the figure of private Sad Sack – a put-upon dogsbody created by a Sergeant George Baker for *Yank*, the army weekly produced both by and for GIs. The magazine

was intended as a morale-booster but faithfully recorded the experiences, dreams – and gripes – of its contributors.

The GIs provided a favourite theme for cartoonists in Britain. Carl Giles (better known as plain 'Giles') often depicted American servicemen in England: smiling, cigar-chomping GIs in their sloppy field jackets, forever hogging taxis and on the look out for souvenirs. Giles joined the *Daily Express* in 1943, and quickly won a wide following for his scenes of daily life on the home front. 'Now I want you to promise me you're all going to be really good little evacuees and not worry his Lordship', runs the caption as a group of villainous evacuee children prepare to overrun a stately home. The *Daily Mirror* provided humour of a saucier kind in the strip-cartoon character

HEAVE HO Hitler is toppled into the abyss by British and American soldiers.

'Jane', who often appeared scantily clad, fretting about her state of undress. Jane was a favourite pin-up. Her admirers had extra cause to rejoice on May 8, 1945, the day of Victory in Europe: the *Daily Mirror* celebrated by showing her, for the first time, completely naked.

AMBUSH A German truck is stopped by members of the French Resistance. Right: members of the right-wing *Milice*, or Militia, round up *maquis* men while (left) an anti-Resistance poster describes Free French fighters as assassins.

ILS ASSASSINENT!
ENVELOPPES DANS LES PLIS DE
NOTRE DRAPEAU

quantities of women's underclothing.

On the night of June 5, 1944, as the vast armada of warships and troop carriers assembled in the English ports for the D-Day landings, the BBC broadcast coded action messages to resistance groups across the Channel – 'The dice are on the table' was one of them – to alert the secret armies for the forthcoming invasion. It was the signal for a massive campaign of sabotage in France, the goal being to disrupt communications and stop the Germans from moving troops to the fighting front.

Telegraph and telephone lines were cut. Bridges, railways and power stations were blown up. Barricades were thrown up to block thoroughfares and road signs painted black to confuse the Germans.

Increasingly, now, the Resistance would act as an irregular wing of the Allied armies. Armed raids and assassinations increased: on country roads, wire was stretched between trees to decapitate approaching German motor cyclists. In city streets, knives were slipped between the ribs of German soldiers and their bodies were dumped in rivers.

EVERYDAY LIFE ON THE EASTERN FRONT

Russian refugees flee the advancing Germans. 'If ten thousand Russian females die
of exhaustion digging an anti-tank ditch for us, that interests me only in as far as
the ditch is dug', declared SS chief Heinrich Himmler. The war on the Eastern Front
was fought with terrible ferocity and losses in the battles were enormous. Meanwhile,
on the home front, appalling suffering was endured by those in the ghettos,
the cities under siege and the concentration camps.

THE PEOPLE'S WAR

'One day an actor just fell dead on the stage. We shuffled in front of him to hide him,

and someone just pulled him into the wings. You had to keep going ...'

– Grigory Polyachik, theatre producer, on the Leningrad famine.

THE RUSSIANS were caught off-guard by Operation Barbarossa – the German invasion that came in June 1941. But preparations were made quickly as the Germans advanced. Sandbags were heaped in mountains against the walls of important public buildings to protect them in air raids and barrage balloons loomed in the skies overhead. For camouflage, the gold onion domes of the Kremlin were painted battleship grey, while the famous Bolshoi Theatre was hung with canvas decorated with false doorways so that it could not be recognised from the air.

In July, 80,000 of Moscow's women and children were evacuated to the east. Parents staying in the capital scrawled names and addresses on their children's hands, but as the evacuees were usually given baths on arrival at their new homes the information was, more often than not, washed off. Those children who stayed in Moscow were often to be seen playing with the boxes of sand and barrels of water which stood on every street corner to be used against fires.

Moscow's Metro stations doubled as air-raid shelters. Some were equipped with small libraries for the civilians sheltering there, complete with benches and books which had to be signed for and returned when the all-clear went.

During lunch hours, parks were thronged with civilians who had emerged from their office blocks and workshops to go through rifle drill. When the day shift ended they could often be seen going out with spades over their shoulders to 'dig for victory' in allotments and town squares.

The story of war production in the Soviet Union is one of the epics of World War II. As the Germans continued their advance on Moscow, the decision was taken to remove vital installations from their path and rebuild them in and beyond the Urals. Whole factories, with their plant, workers and families, were shifted hundreds of miles to the east. The mass exodus from Moscow began in October 1941, when factory workers laboured night and day to unbolt their crucial machinery, load it into numbered crates and heave it into railway trucks where it was camouflaged with birch twigs.

A NEW WORKFORCE

The dismantled factories reappeared at Magnitogorsk, Cheliabinsk, Omutninsk and other distant sites. Hordes of people went with them, choking the trains with their children and bundled belongings. By the end of 1941 about 1500 factories had been moved, with 10 million people to work in them. New towns were built, and new oil and mineral reserves were developed. That year Soviet tank production doubled while aircraft numbers trebled. By 1945 the Soviet Union had turned out as much weaponry as Nazi Germany – and outstripped Hitler's Reich in tank and aircraft manufacture.

To boost Soviet war production, women were mobilised as nowhere else. They took men's places in the very toughest of industrial work – sweltering in the open-hearth workshops, the rolling mills and smelting ovens of the steelworks, for example. They were also employed in snow and frost, digging ditches

SCENES FROM SOVIET RUSSIA

Tobacco was rationed in Russia as elsewhere. In Moscow, black marketeers with cigarettes stood in the streets charging passers-by two roubles for every single puff.

During the war, Stalin was so keen to improve relations with his capitalist allies that the famous revolutionary call to arms – the Internationale – was replaced as the Soviet Union's national anthem in January 1944.

CITIES UNDER SIEGE Hauling away the dead in Leningrad, 1941.
Right: thousands of Muscovites were evacuated, but for those left behind,
the capital's Underground system was used to shelter from air raids.

SOVIET PROPAGANDA Wall posters in Russia conveyed simple, powerful messages. Above: a worker and soldier are united through arms manufacture. Far left: smashing a German signpost that points 'To the East'.

around Moscow and other cities.

As the war progressed, the armed forces soaked up ever more men and by 1945 there were more women than men in the Soviet civilian workforce. Even children were mobilised for the work front. They were put to use in the many school workshops which turned out gun parts and packing cases for munitions factories as well as rainproof clothes for the soldiers, sheets and pillowcases for hospitals, and so on.

THE PROPAGANDA WAR

A huge propaganda effort accompanied the struggle, and radio played a key role in a country where millions could neither read nor write. Public announcements crackled out through loudspeakers on street corners in the cities. In the vast rural areas, radio receivers were set up in communal 'reading huts'. These were roughly built shelters where the peasants gathered to listen to propaganda broadcasts and to hear the latest updates on rationing and food availability. Receivers were also installed in museums, parks, clubs, dormitories and hospitals.

It was over Moscow Radio that Stalin broadcast to the people at 6.30 on the morning of Thursday, July 3, 1941 – the first time that the remote, awe-inspiring

figure had spoken to the Soviet people since 1938. In the capital, crowds filled Red Square and Stalin's message was carried by amplifiers all over Moscow.

'Brothers and sisters, friends', were the dictator's opening words, delivered in a voice clearly touched with emotion. He went on to appeal to people's courage and patriotism, and issued the now-famous orders for scorched-earth and partisan action. Not a single kilogram of grain or litre of petrol was to be left for the enemy. In occupied areas, partisan units must blow up bridges, destroy roads, telephones and telegraph wires, and set fire to forests, enemy stores and road convoys.

The writer Konstantin Simonov has described the impact of the speech. 'Stalin spoke in a slow, toneless voice, with a strong Georgian accent. Once or twice you could hear a glass clink as he drank water. His voice was low and soft, and might have seemed perfectly calm, but for his heavy, tired breathing and that water he was drinking.'

The resolve in his voice was undeniable, and people came to respect it. 'They loved him in different ways, wholeheartedly or with

reservations; admiring him and yet fearing him; and some didn't like him at all. But nobody doubted his courage and his iron will.'

Besides the radio, brightly coloured posters proved an invaluable means of boosting morale and communicating simple ideas to the illiterate. Soviet artists had already made themselves masters of this propaganda form. The first war poster appeared on the streets of Moscow the day after the German invasion, with the typically forthright caption: 'We Shall Crush and Exterminate the Fascist Viper.' Hundreds more followed, savagely caricaturing the Nazi leaders, displaying heroic Soviet figures, exposing German atrocities and depicting giant Russian pincers tightening around the enemy throat. Another distinctive Russian device was the propaganda train – a locomotive with carriages converted into moving cinemas or printing works. Manned by lecturers, actors and artists, these trains steamed across the nation with speeches and war bulletins.

The cinema too made an enormous contribution. While newsreel cameramen sent back footage from every front, patriotic films were revived to strengthen resolve. None is more famous than *Alexander Nevsky* (1938), a medieval tale about a Russian prince who defeats invading Teutonic knights in a battle on the ice of Lake Peipus. Among the films made during the war was *Zoya* (1944), about a real-life partisan girl who was captured, tortured and hanged while working behind German lines. In Moscow, cinema projectors were installed in some of the big Metro stations, providing film shows for people sheltering there from German bombs.

Songs played their part in the war effort. After it was first performed by the Red Army Ensemble in June 1941, *Sacred War* became the theme song for Moscow Radio when it came on in the morning. During public performances, people rose from their

RUSSIAN HOME FRONT The aftermath of a German air raid on Leningrad.
Left: Russian women dig trenches to hinder the German advance.
Right: the face of hunger – a Leningrad man cherishes a crust of bread.

HARDSHIP In besieged Leningrad people kept in touch with events by radio. Right: men and women resistance fighters pause for food in the Russian countryside, 1942.

seats and stood in silence until the music ended.

The scale of the suffering in the Soviet Union matched the immensity of the war effort. The Nazi leadership regarded all Slavs as subhumans and treated their opponents with ferocious contempt. 'It will be a war of extermination,' Hitler had predicted. 'In the East, cruelty is a boon.' Russian prisoners of war caught behind enemy lines by the speed of the advance were left to starve to death in droves, while civilians became a convenient source of slave labour.

The battles were colossal – almost unimaginable – in their dimensions. Over a million people died at Stalingrad in a heavyweight clash that became a byword for close-combat savagery. On the home front, too, the suffering was immense. More than 1.5 million people perished in the three-year defence of Leningrad, for example. At the height of the siege some 10,000 of the city's inhabitants died of starvation every day. Writer Vera Ketlivskaya sat in her apartment with the temperature so low that the ink froze in the inkwell while she was working on her book *The Blockade*. In the next room lay her mother, dead of starvation, placed on the floor three days before, with no immediate hope of getting her buried. One elderly artist strangled his pet cat and ate it. Later he tried to hang himself but the rope snapped; he fell to the floor, broke his leg and froze to death. People in Leningrad ate anything they could get hold of, even scraping paper off the walls to suck at the glue.

In town and country alike, the distinction between home and war fronts was often blurred, for the Germans overran vast tracts of land which were hard to control, and where ragged irregular armies waged guerrilla war against the occupiers. The partisans crossed and recrossed the long fighting front by remote paths through swamp and forest, moving through landscapes of burnt towns and villages, plagued by hunger, cold, damp, lice and scurvy.

The partisans found willing helpers among the civilian population. Advice and encouragement came in the form of a book almost 500 pages long which was dropped in masses behind enemy lines. Called *The Partisan's Companion*, it gave tips on everything from blowing up railways and survival techniques in the steppe to recipes for appetising dishes made from mushrooms, bilberries and hedgehogs. Village children would scour fields and forests to look for dud shells from which gunpowder was obtained to manufacture home-made mines. In towns, lemonade factories were given over to the manufacture of Molotov cocktails – the crude but effective petrol bombs that took their name from the Soviet foreign minister.

Atrocities were committed on both sides in the partisan war. And reprisals were taken on a horrific scale throughout Eastern Europe. But the shooting of hostages became so widespread and random that it ultimately failed as a deterrent. German demands were frankly impossible for ordinary people to meet – whether people tried to comply or offered resistance, they seemed to be equally at risk.

EASTERN EUROPE

From the destruction of Lidice in Czechoslovakia to the ultimate horrors of

Auschwitz and Treblinka, Eastern Europe witnessed the extremities of wartime suffering.

Six million men, women and children perished in concentration camps.

AMONG ALL THE COUNTRIES overrun by Hitler's troops, none suffered worse than Poland. It became a plunderground and a terror zone. Part of the country was simply incorporated into the Reich and destined for ruthless 'Germanisation'. But the remainder – the eastern part of Poland – was ruled by a Governor, Hans Frank, and his cabinet according to patterns of unlimited exploitation.

All its raw materials and industrial machinery were seized for the use of the German war economy, and the only enterprises allowed to remain functioning were those needed to keep the population at bare subsistence level. While the inhabitants were employed as a gigantic forced-labour reservoir, the country also served as a dumping ground for a variety of 'undesirable elements' from the Reich. Much of the holocaust of Europe's Jews took place on Polish soil.

The demoralisation of the Poles was planned with care. Polish men between 18 and 25 years of age were drafted early on into a labour force called the *Baudienst*, where they worked under military discipline for next to no pay. All Polish workers could, in principle, be directed to work wherever the authorities chose; and, besides being expected to survive on pitiful rations, the population was denied education. Hardly anything except primary schooling was permitted. Poles were only expected to be able to sign their names, count to 500 and learn that it was God's will that they should be polite and obedient to their German masters.

But if the Poles themselves were treated as barely human, the plight of the country's large Jewish population was even worse. The Nazis first crammed as many Jews as they could find into walled-off ghettos in cities. The largest of these was the Warsaw Ghetto which contained nearly half a million people; here they lived dozens to a room or even slept in the street, where the inhabitants had to pick their way among the corpses of those who had died from malnutrition.

It was from ghettos like this that hundreds of thousands of Jews were transferred in truckloads to the concentration camps. Rumours of their mass murder were finally confirmed when the Resistance was able to extract a sample from three railway carriage-loads of human hair from the Treblinka camp. Chemical analysis revealed that the hair came from people who had been killed by a gas containing hydrogen cyanide.

In the Warsaw Ghetto, the remaining Jews decided

A FINAL ACT OF RESISTANCE

Resistance went on even in the concentration camps. At Mauthausen, prisoners sweated all day in a deep quarry and it was the practice for those who could stand it no longer to go to the top and jump off. Two Jewish brothers decided to take their lives and shook hands with their friends before making the climb. At the top they met two SS guards and shook hands with them too – they held on tight and jumped, each taking an oppressor with him.

LIQUIDATION
In some areas special SS units called *Einsatzgruppen* 'task forces' were used to kill Jews.

FACE OF FEAR German troops round up civilians in the Warsaw Ghetto, where almost 500,000 people lived.

on militant resistance and on April 19, 1943, when the SS entered to round up more victims, they were met with gunfire. Incredibly, the half-starved and ill-equipped inhabitants managed to hold out until May while the Germans bombed, shelled and burned the ghetto to the ground. About 100 Jews escaped through the sewers with the aid of Resistance workers. But the rest either died in the fighting or ended up in the camps.

INDUSTRIALISED EVIL

Many Jews were suffocated in the cattle trucks used for transportation. Those who survived the journey but were too weak to work found themselves in the death camps – places of extermination where they were not expected to live more than 24 hours after arrival. Treblinka, Chelmno, Sobibor, Majdanek, Belzec and Birkenau (the death camp attached to Auschwitz work camp) simply fed their human freight into what were referred to as 'showers'. The victims went in naked, as many as 2000 to a room. Then the doors were barred and the fumes from Zyklon-B crystals began to pour through the ventilation shafts.

Those destined for the work camps were stripped on arrival, disinfected, numbered by tattoo and made

HANDS OUT OF POCKETS

The German authorities in Poland became paranoid about attacks by Resistance groups. In October 1943, during a meeting of the General Government cabinet, it was suggested that the law should forbid civilians from keeping their hands in their pockets. Certainly, it was argued, 'Armed and uniformed Germans should be prepared to use firearms whenever a civilian, with hands in his pockets, is coming near them'.

'THIS MUST BE THE CAMP'

POLAND, 1944

❝ Towards eleven o'clock, the train began to move. We pressed against the windows. The convoy was moving slowly. A quarter of an hour later, it slowed down again. Through the windows we could see barbed wire; we realized that this must be the camp.

We had forgotten the existence of Madame Schächter. Suddenly, we heard terrible screams: "Jews, look! Look through the window! Flames! Look!"

And as the train stopped, we saw this time that flames were gushing out of a tall chimney, into the black sky. Madame Schächter was silent herself. Once more she had become dumb, indifferent, absent, and had gone back to her corner. We looked at the flames in the darkness. There was an abominable odour floating in the air. Suddenly, our doors opened. Some odd-looking characters, dressed in striped shirts and black trousers, leapt into the wagon. They held electric torches and truncheons. They began to strike out to right and left, shouting: "Everybody get out! Everyone out of the wagon! Quickly!"

We jumped out. I threw a last glance towards Madame Schächter. Her little boy was holding her hand.

In front of us, flames. In the air that smell of burning flesh. It must have been about midnight. We had arrived. At Birkenau reception centre for Auschwitz. ❞

From the recollections of Elie Wiesel, concentration-camp survivor.

HUMAN FREIGHT Prisoners were transported to the camps in cattle trucks.

to wear striped convict clothing which removed any remaining shred of human dignity. The different types of prisoner were identified by coloured triangles: pink for homosexual; red for political (often Communists); green for criminal; and so on. Jews wore the yellow star of David.

Accommodation was in bleak huts where the prisoners slept at night, often on dysentery-fouled bunks or tiers of shelves, shivering under inadequate blankets. During the day the prisoners worked, often in parties sent out of the camp to toil in quarries, factories and mines. In the evening, the working parties returned to the camp carrying their dead with them.

Some escapes were made, but for a single success hundreds of prisoners might be made to stand in the compound, naked and motionless, for a whole winter's night. By morning, many would have frozen to death. The corpses of concentration-camp victims were burnt in the furnaces of crematoria whose chimneys belched an acrid, distinctive smoke.

The whole operation was run for profit – and not only through fees earned by the hiring out of slave labour. Clothes, jewellery and other belongings were sold by the SS. Human hair shaved from the heads of those destined to die was used to stuff pillows and mattresses, and to make slippers for U-boat crewmen. Gold teeth and fillings were picked from the mouths of the

DESTITUTION Jews in the Warsaw Ghetto were kept on starvation rations.

dead and collected to swell the coffers of a special SS bank account.

Altogether, six million men, women and children were martyred by the industrialised evil of the concentration camp system.

THE HEAVY HAND OF OPPRESSION

While Poland and occupied Russia succumbed to the full force of the Nazi terror, other countries of eastern and central Europe also felt the heavy hand of oppression. Czechoslovakia, for example, had been seized by the Germans in 1939, becoming a protectorate of the Reich. Student demonstrations led the Germans to ban all higher and secondary education, and with continued unrest Reinhard Heydrich was installed in September 1941 as *Reichsprotektor,* or imperial governor. Second man in the SS, he was Himmler's leading henchman. Arrests and executions quickly became widespread in Czechoslovakia, and the Resistance laid plans for Heydrich's assassination. On May 27, 1942, a Czech agent threw a bomb into Heydrich's Mercedes – he died later in hospital. The Nazis took a horrific revenge for the assassination. All the male inhabitants of the village of Lidice, near Prague, were shot and the women and children deported to concentration camps. The village was razed and ploughed over, its name even removed from the map. A similar fate befell the smaller village of Lezaky nearby, and subsequently the whole Czech underground was effectively stifled.

Elsewhere in eastern and central Europe, an assortment of dictators formed uneasy alliances with Hitler. Romania and Bulgaria, for example, aligned themselves with the Axis powers. In Hungary, the regent Admiral Miklos Horthy did the same, and he retained some limited authority even when the Germans occupied his country in March 1944. The invaders did, however, round up and deport for slave labour or the gas chambers some 400,000 out of 800,000 Hungarian Jews. In October 1944, when Horthy tried to negotiate a surrender with Russia, the Germans had him bundled off to a concentration camp too, and Hungary endured a terrible martyrdom, Budapest being sacked by both Germans and Russians.

Greece and Yugoslavia were both ravaged by the enmity of rival partisan armies – Communist and non-Communist – who fought each other as well as the Axis enemy. In Yugoslavia, medical supplies were in such short supply that bandages were sometimes taken from the dying, rinsed in streams and used again on the living. It was in every sense a dirty war, and the scale of reprisals was appalling. At Kraguvejac in Yugoslavia 5000 male hostages were shot in one day in October 1941.

COST OF RESISTANCE The Czech village of Lidice was destroyed in retaliation for the death of Heydrich, seen in the centre of the picture (right). The children of Lidice (above) were deported to concentration camps.

THE AXIS POWERS: BEHIND ENEMY LINES

Mass rallies ... ceaseless propaganda ... secret police terror ... indoctrination of the

young ... all of these were familiar features of daily existence in the dictatorships.

Totalitarian government stamped national life with a unique character in Germany,

Italy and Japan: the three powers known as the Axis who were united

by a pact of 1940. Yet other aspects of everyday life, such as gas masks and

ration cards, would have been familiar on the Allied Home Front.

INSIDE THE REICH

'I swear by God this holy oath, that I will render to Adolf Hitler, Leader of the German

nation and people, Supreme Commander of the Armed Forces, unconditional obedience'

– a German oath of allegiance.

FOR GERMAN FAMILIES living under the threat of mass bombing, many experiences of everyday living were similar to those known in Britain. The blackout was strictly enforced, for example, and people had to get used to finding their way round in the dark, sometimes wearing luminous patches or using feebly glowing torches. Gas masks were issued and German children, like their British counterparts, took furtive delight in blowing rude noises through their rubbery cheek pieces.

Curious-looking hand-sirens, mounted on tripods, were distributed to towns and villages to warn of air raids. There was also a device called the *Drahtfunk* (cable radio) attached to the family wireless set which was kept switched on and went 'ping pong' whenever enemy bombers approached.

During the first week of war, ration cards were delivered to houses by Nazi officials. There were blue cards for meat, red for groceries, pink for bread and flour, and yellow for butter and other fats. Children under 16 years received double rations of butter. The weekly meat ration was 16oz (450g) per person – somewhat less than the British allocation. Foul-tasting *ersatz* (substitute) coffee was one of the most memorable introductions, made from acorns and billed as *gesund, starkend und schmackhaft* ('healthy, strength-giving and tasty'). A soap that made lather only after much effort and a tobacco likened to low-grade mattress-filling also made their appearance.

In Hitler's Reich, as elsewhere, people gave up garden railings to help the war effort. Once a week children carried bags of scrap iron, silver paper, rags, bones, waste paper and other materials into school where they were carefully weighed. Points were awarded, and those who had most points were given a rousing cheer by their schoolmates.

In the early days, however, the mass of the people experienced no great hardship. Through the euphoric year of 1940, German soldiers started coming home on leave, brown and fit from their devastating *Blitzkrieg* victories, and all sorts of foreign luxuries found their way into German homes: furs from Norway; coffee, chocolate and tea from Holland and Belgium; perfume and lingerie from France.

The Nazi Government positively encouraged extravagant enjoyment during this period, and the

---

EYEWITNESS

'DON'T YOU KNOW THE GERMAN GREETING?'
DÜSSELDORF, 1940

❛ One thing [this teacher] did like to receive from us was "Heil Hitler!" Every day we had to greet her, and other grown-ups, with the salute. I was used to doing this, but it still embarrassed me. On my way to school one day I went into a busy shop without making the greeting, thinking no one would notice. But a shop assistant pounced on me, saying angrily, "Don't you know the German greeting?" She made me walk out and come back into the shop again, using the right greeting. I must have blushed to the roots of my long plaited hair as I held my arm out and said "Heil Hitler!" in a pretend grown-up voice. Then she started talking loudly to the other customers about children's bad manners nowadays. ❜

From the recollections of Elsbeth Emmerich, a German schoolgirl.

YOUNG GERMANS Josef Goebbels greets Hitler Youth members. Right: a poster for a 'World Meeting of Hitler Youth'. Left: the magazine *The Week* shows a girl harvester.

newsreels playing in packed cinemas at Christmas showed propaganda minister Josef Goebbels handing out parcels like Santa Claus. There was immense relief that the war seemed to have ended so quickly for, despite the Führer's grandiose ambitions for his Reich, the German economy was not geared up for anything more than a short, sharp war. No preparations had been made for the long struggle that was to come.

Factories were still turning out peacetime consumer goods. Though petrol rationing allowed fuel only for vehicles used in the national interest, magazines still featured the new Volkswagen ('people's car'), which cost 975 marks and could be bought on an easy purchase system with weekly payments of 5 marks. It was envisaged that there would be hundreds of thousands of them after the war. Hitler's aim was to put his nation on wheels as Henry Ford had done in the United States (motorway-building was pioneered in Hitler's Germany – the Reich had 2300 miles of Autobahn before World War II broke out).

For millions throughout the Fatherland, Hitler was a focus of loyalty bordering on religious devotion. To a defeated nation, riven by bitterness and unrest, he had brought order and a new sense of collective pride. Massive unemployment had been solved by the Nazis' vast programme of public works. At the gigantic public rallies staged by the Reich in peacetime, Hitler appeared to the people as saviour, sorcerer – even messiah.

THE HITLER YOUTH

The cult of the Führer had, however, eroded precious individual liberties. In Hitler's Reich, democratic elections had long since ceased to exist. The Gestapo, or secret police, had access to people's private lives on a disquieting scale and to oppose the Nazi authorities invited denunciation by anyone from a next-door neighbour to a local member of the Hitler Youth or the *Bund Deutscher Mädchen* (German Girls' League). Denunciations of parents, even, by their own children were not unknown.

The Nazis paid particular attention to the indoctrination of young Germans, who were marched and drilled and taught Party songs in the youth movements. Physical fitness was especially prized, as

EATING AND DRINKING

Eating habits were transformed everywhere by wartime shortages, synthetic foods and rationing.

IN MANY COUNTRIES where food rationing was introduced, the health of the civilian population improved. In Britain, for example, the poor fared better than they had in peacetime because of government encouragement to eat healthy, vitamin-rich foods. Pregnant women were supplied with milk and orange juice so that fewer mothers died in childbirth. And Lord Woolton, the Minister of Food, ensured that every British child got daily milk, cod-liver oil and orange juice, too, to boost vitamin intake. Everyone may have been a little hungry in wartime Britain, but no one starved.

Nor did rationing prove a great affliction in Hitler's Reich. It is reckoned that about 40 per cent of the German population actually found themselves better fed – particularly in the early years of the war – than they had been in the 1930s.

There were some notable differences between Britain and Germany in the way food was allocated. Bread, for example, was never rationed in Britain during the course of the war but it was restricted in Germany to about 1½lb (725g) per adult per week.

There was no milk ration in Germany as there was in Britain. But in other respects, the diets were fairly similar: in both countries, people had to make do with an average of half a real egg per week during the middle years of the war. Rations varied considerably, however, even within individual nations. For example, the British cheese ration of 1oz (30g) per week on May 5, 1941, had grown to 8oz (225g) by July 26, 1942.

RELIEF OPERATION Soviet troops distribute bread to Germans, May 1945. Hunger began to bite in the Reich only towards the end of the war.

GERMAN RATIONS The average weekly quantities per person in the war's middle years: bread, eggs, meat, butter, margarine, edible oil, ersatz or substitute coffee, cheese, sugar and jam. Milk was unrationed.

BRITISH RATIONS The average weekly quantities per person of milk, eggs, meat, butter, margarine, edible oil, tea, cheese, sugar, jam. As was the case in Germany, the meat ration worked out at roughly 1lb (500g) a week.

EAT NUTRITIONAL FOOD ★ ★ U.S. NEEDS US STRONG

Every day, eat this way

MILK & MILK PRODUCTS...
at least a pint for everyone—more for children—or cheese or evaporated or dried milk.

BREAD & CEREAL...whole grain products or enriched white bread and flour.

ORANGES, TOMATOES, GRAPEFRUIT
...or raw cabbage or salad greens—at least one of these.

MEAT, POULTRY or FISH
...dried beans, peas or nuts occasionally.

Green or Yellow VEGETABLES
...one big helping or more —some raw, some cooked.

EGGS ... at least 3 or 4 a week, cooked any way you choose—or in "made" dishes.

OTHER VEGETABLES, FRUIT
...potatoes, other vegetables or fruits in season.

BUTTER & OTHER SPREADS
...vitamin-rich fats, peanut butter, and similar spreads.

Then eat other foods you also like

Property of Federal Security Agency—may be reproduced by permission only

OFFICE OF DEFENSE HEALTH AND WELFARE SERVICES, PAUL V. McNUTT, DIRECTOR, WASHINGTON, D. C.

HEALTHY APPETITES Wartime shopping in the United States. Above: the advertisement promotes healthy eating.

Watching the changes and making the best of supplies were essential skills for housewives everywhere. People bargained, cajoled, haggled and swapped. A Californian woman reported: 'I remember all the neighbourhood women sitting around the kitchen table pooling and trading coupons. My grandmother raised chickens so we often didn't need our meat coupons. And we made our own butter. So one month we might trade our sugar for steak and nylons. I know rationing was sometimes a hardship to my mother, but as a child seeing all these coupons trading back and forth, it was like a big Monopoly game.'

SOUP KITCHEN Italian children are fed at a refugee centre after the liberation.

FROSTY RECEPTION Hungry Parisians buying apples at an open-air stall in near-zero temperatures, January 1945.

HOME FRONT HAIRDOS

To maintain an atmosphere of success, Nazi propagandists encouraged luxuries on the home front. Fancy permanent-wave hairdos, for example, were frowned on in wartime Britain. But German armaments minister Albert Speer was repeatedly blocked in his attempts to ban them – and the manufacture of cosmetics – by Hitler himself, under the influence of his mistress, Eva Braun.

was 'hardness'. Character-building mottoes, written on blackboards for children to copy in their exercise books, included 'A German should be tough as leather, quick as a greyhound, and hard as Krupp steel'. At Hitler Youth camps the strength of a member's will power could be confirmed by eating a tin of boot polish.

Members of the Girls' League were taught all about Hitler's life and went on youth hostel weekends where they were made to run 60 metres in 12 seconds, swim 100 metres and throw a ball over 20 metres. *Kraft durch Freude* ('Strength through Joy') was the great slogan of the Nazi organisation promoting sporting activities, vacations and excursions.

'You are Nothing, the *Volk* [People] is Everything' was another favourite Nazi motto. And there can be no doubt that many children enjoyed the team-spiritedness, the marching and the songs as well as the colourful paraphernalia of banners, uniforms, badges and lanyards. What they lost, under the intense pressure to conform, was the opportunity to develop a critical adult intelligence. Deviation from Nazi norms quickly brought mockery and humiliation. Among adults, it led swiftly to the sinister attentions of the Party officials – or of the Gestapo.

Teachers and all other people in state jobs had to be members of the Party. Elsbeth Emmerich, a schoolgirl in wartime Germany, described how pressure was routinely applied. Her mother, a keen sportswoman, took up coaching young athletes during the early war years. Not long after, there was a knock at the door.

'Enter a stranger. A strange man with notebook and pencil and a Nazi pin in his lapel. He said that he'd heard about my mother and her achievements. He had assumed that she was a member of the Party and only found out that she was not when he checked his records.' (Of course, anyone who referred to the Party meant the Nazi Party, there was only one.)

'No doubt that was just an oversight, he went on, and would she join? He had his pencil at the ready but my mother froze over and said firmly "NO". She did not want to become a member of the Party. He wanted to know her reasons, and she said that she had reasons of her own. He didn't understand.

' "You realise you cannot keep your position as coach to our young girls, unless you are a member of the Party?" My mum said surely coaching had nothing to do with politics, and that being a Party member would not make her a better coach. However, the man with the Party

GETTING READY Blackout drill and gas-mask practice were as much features of German life as of life in the Allied nations.
Far left: a poster urges 'Build Youth Hostels'.

WARTIME MOTIFS A scene from *Die Grosse Liebe* (The Great Love) made in 1942 and the most popular wartime film. Right: the songsheet from a film praising the role of the Luftwaffe.

THE NAZIS took the cinema very seriously as a propaganda medium – so seriously that in 1939, the destruction of Gdynia in Poland was delayed to give the cameramen time to get forward and film the advancing German troops from the front. Long before the war broke out, Leni Riefenstahl had created a classic propaganda film in *Triumph of the Will*, about the 1934 Nuremberg Rally. In the opening sequence the Führer is shown descending by plane from the skies. Later come mesmerising rally scenes of drilled masses and rapt spectators, all embodying collective purpose and discipline against the backdrop of three giant swastika banners.

In 1940, the infamous *Jud Süss* appeared – the epitome of anti-Semitic propaganda. It was set in the 18th century and tells the story of an evil tax collector, Süss Oppenheimer, who forces a German maiden to choose between letting him ravish her or having her lover broken on the wheel.

The documentaries celebrating German victories in the *Blitzkrieg* included *Sieg im Westen* (Victory in the West). Films like this were considered so important that a law was passed forbidding anyone to leave or enter a cinema during the showing of a war documentary.

Not all films had an obvious propaganda purpose. The German UFA studios also churned out a stream of escapist comedies and musicals. But output declined as the war entered its final phase.

The last feature film made by UFA was *Kolberg* – an historical drama about a Prussian garrison's heroic resistance to Napoleon's armies and, in order to make the film, two German divisions were withdrawn from the disintegrating Eastern Front.

CAMERA CREW A German film cameraman enters the Warsaw Ghetto under escort.

MOTHER AND SON This German wears the *Mutterkreuz,* or 'Cross of Motherhood', awarded to mothers with large families for their service to the Reich.

pin in his lapel knew better and my mother had to give up a much cherished job.'

People were reprimanded for failing to give the Heil Hitler salute. Names were taken of householders who did not have the obligatory portrait of the Führer on their walls. Failure to put out a Nazi flag on Hitler's birthday brought a knock at the door.

Quite apart from the nightmares of the Gestapo cells and concentration camps, the first of which was set up in Germany in 1933, daily life under the Third Reich was irksome and restrictive in a multitude of ways. The young women, for example, made hard and fit by their training in the Girls' League, were then relegated to the kitchen by a Nazi ideology that

believed their only role was to be a housewife. Women held no leading positions in the party hierarchy. Married women doctors and civil servants were dismissed from their posts. Under Nazism, German women were ineligible for jury service.

There was, however, massive official encouragement to bear children for the Fatherland – even if the mother was unmarried – and a 'Cross of Motherhood' was awarded to women with large families. Ernst Kaltenbrunner of the SS announced: 'All single and married women up to the age of thirty-five who do not already have four children should be obliged to produce four children by racially pure, exceptionable German men. Whether these men are married is without significance.' Eugenics – the attempt to improve the German race by controlled, selective breeding – created all kinds of problems. Some German women shunned marriage because of the sheer amount of paperwork involved in certifying their Aryan ancestry.

FOR ARYANS ONLY

Gipsies, Communists, homosexuals and Jehovah's Witnesses were just a few of the groups marginalised and persecuted by the Reich authorities. But none suffered more than the Jews, whose martyrdom in Germany began long before war broke out.

The Nazis' racial laws officially sanctioned acts of vandalism and violence against them, and there was no redress. In a famous photograph from peacetime Germany, the Munich lawyer Dr Spiegel was shown walking barefoot through the streets of his city –

'SOME COULD NOT BEAR THE SIGHT OF US'

LEHRTE, 1944

❢ Our swastikas on the map kept on retreating from the eastern front. Kiev was back in Russian hands, and the Red Army was in Estonia, nearing the Polish frontier ... Twice a week the Hitler Youth had "Station Duty". We dished out cold and hot drinks to the homeless who crowded the platforms, and when a Red Cross train stopped, we took large jugs with malt-coffee or hot soup into the trains, and handed them to the soldiers in their bunk beds. Their blood-stained bandages and the stench made me feel sick, but their sad, haggard faces made us forget our nausea. We tried to cheer them up. The response was varied; some still had some humour left, some eyed us silently but gratefully for the food and drink we had given them, some could not bear the sight of us in the Hitler Youth uniform. ❢

From the recollections of Renate Greenshields, a pastor's daughter.

HEIL HITLER
Germans in the
Baltic states
swear allegiance.
The poster
proclaims 'One
People, One
Nation, One
Leader'.

Ein Volk, ein Reich, ein Führer!

followed by Stormtroopers – with a placard around his neck. 'I shall never complain to the police again', read the text.

Jews were banned from the medical profession, from university posts and legal offices. Signs in municipal parks and on public benches announced, 'For Aryans Only'. Marriage between Jews and people of German blood was forbidden.

ANTI-SEMITISM The poster advertises a propaganda film, *The Eternal Jew,* while (right) a stormtrooper helps to enforce the boycott of Jewish shops. Below right: premises wrecked during the *Kristallnacht* of 1938.

Street posters called for the boycott of Jewish shops, and the climax of the pre-war persecution was the nationwide violence of the *Kristallnacht* (Night of Broken Glass) when Jewish-owned shops were smashed and synagogues burnt to the ground.

In 1941 things went further. It was decreed that all Jews in Germany over the age of six were forbidden to appear in public without a yellow Jewish star bearing the inscription 'Jew' in black. 'It is to be worn on the left breast of the clothing, clearly visible and strongly sewn on.'

The decree brought surprises. 'I must tell you what a shock my boss got when I turned up wearing the Jew's Star,' recalled one half-Jewish woman who worked for a staunchly Nazi firm of picture-framers which sold portraits of Hitler and other Party leaders.

'I can still see their astonished faces today when they heard that their model German working girl was really born of "that lazy race of parasites that were feeding off the body of the German people". They didn't say a word as I packed up my things; they just stared at me ...' Made to join a Jewish forced-labour squad, she was transported the next year to the concentration camp at Auschwitz.

The extermination camps were located in Poland, but even in Germany there were many concentration camps – places of mass imprisonment – that became death centres later in the war: Bergen-Belsen,

'TROOPS HAVE MADE BRUNSWICK THEIR TARGET'

OCTOBER 15, 1944: MIDNIGHT

❝ Strong contingents of British and American troops have made Brunswick their target and tonight have destroyed almost the whole of the town centre with its mediaeval, half-timbered houses. It was a sea of fire, burning for days. We weren't much better off out in the suburbs and had to stay in the dark shelter until daylight dawned. The asphalt on the streets is glowing red-hot. The fire brigade had to hose down the pathway so that we could get out. Then we set off through the smoke-laden half-light into the unknown. You could still see the old slogans on the walls that were still standing: "Take Care! The Enemy is listening-in." "You are Nothing, the Volk is Everything." "Give all for the Führer, the People and the Fatherland." "Wheels must turn for Victory." A macabre spectacle ... ❞

From the recollections of Sigrid Wendt, a German housewife.

Ravensbrück, Sachsenhausen, Buchenwald and Dachau were among them.

Few German civilians knew precisely what went on in the camps, but the wartime ordeals of the Jews could not be kept entirely secret. A Düsseldorf housewife wrote in her diary for April 1942, 'Once again there are huge columns of Jews passing our house. The suffering of these poor tottering figures is indescribable. They stop to rest outside our house. They just flop down in the roadway. Many are so exhausted they can't get up again. Often they are too weary to carry their bundles any further, and just leave them lying in the road.

'Mothers comfort crying children. Old men are helped along by sons and daughters. Sheer misery stares out of the eyes of every one of them. I heard a German woman in the street say, "Pray God we never have to answer for this".'

The 'Final Solution' of mass extermination was planned at the Wannsee Conference in January 1942. It was kept secret, but even when whispers about the gas chambers began to circulate, most Germans who heard them preferred not to listen. It was dangerous even to know such things – to talk about them could prove disastrous. And besides, with the Allied bombing campaign stepping up and with worsening news from the Eastern Front, German civilians were facing new problems of their own.

RATIONING, RADIO AND RUBBLE WOMEN

It was in the winter of 1941–2 that shortages on the German home front began to bite, while no amount of propaganda could disguise the fact that the Reich was meeting its first reverses in the field. The government appealed for furs and warm coats to be sent to the soldiers on the Russian front. Bread, meat and fat rations were reduced. And, with more farm workers being called up, potatoes had to be rationed too.

While the daily diet worsened, German housewives got used to making do. 'You could hardly get anything worth having for your clothing coupons,' recalled Sigrid Wendt from Brunswick, 'so we had to find our own solutions. Make eyes at the shopkeeper on the corner and you could get an empty flour or sugar-sack. Sugar-bags were the best for unravelling.

You got piles of shiny, silky

MAKING PROVISIONS
Germans prepare food for families who have lost their homes in Allied bombing raids.

RESISTANCE IN GERMANY

THE VAST popular enthusiasm for Hitler's regime in Germany combined with the power of the Gestapo to make organised resistance very difficult. But some voices were raised in dissent. The Roman Catholic Bishop of Münster, Cardinal Claus von Galen, preached openly against the Nazi policy of euthanasia for the mentally ill – and his opposition was a key factor in getting the programme dropped. After the German defeat at Stalingrad, the so-called 'White Rose' group of dissidents led 4000 students at Munich university in shouting down the Gauleiter (district governor) of Bavaria when he came to address the student body.

Seven thousand Jews managed to survive the war by living underground in Nazi Germany – including about 4000 in Berlin itself. They were dubbed 'U-boats' because of their submerged life, and survived on forged or borrowed papers and ration cards, moving between cellars, cupboards under the stairs, and garden sheds in the homes of the few friends prepared to assist them.

Wartime schoolgirl Renate Ungewitter, whose father was a Lutheran pastor, has described how their vicarage had a secret room where Jews were hidden while she and her brother (both active in the Hitler Youth) helped to watch out for the Gestapo. The fugitives' faces were always thin and pale from worry and lack of fresh air. They might stay for only one night – a week at the most.

'Every time they moved on to the next hideout, a new address was given to them, never more than one address at a time. Continuously they were on the move. I know of one couple who in 18 months went to 66 different houses, but they survived.'

strands which could be knitted or crocheted into lovely pullovers and jackets.'

Also in 1942, Allied strategic bombing offensives began to bring devastation to German cities, with the specific aim of breaking civilian morale. Wounded soldiers started to appear in the streets, and so many troops were killed in action that the newspapers were forbidden to print more than a handful of death notices in each issue.

The radio, always a key instrument of Nazi propaganda, had never been more important. For each block of houses or apartment building there was a 'radio warden' – a Party member whose task was to encourage neighbours to listen to propaganda broadcasts. The radio wardens sometimes lent money to help people to buy wireless sets, and also reported on people's reactions to the latest speeches.

Now, as people came to doubt the inevitability of victory and to question official versions of the war's progress, more and more Germans tuned in to the foreign stations – especially the BBC. Harsh prison sentences (and even the death penalty) were meted out to those found guilty of listening to foreign broadcasts. The local radio warden had the job of reporting offenders.

Crouching over their sets, with the volume at barely audible levels, millions of Germans defied the government prohibition. As the war progressed, the news worsened. January 1943 brought the crushing German defeat at Stalingrad – the turning point of the war – when 300,000 starving Wehrmacht men were killed or captured.

GERMAN RATIONS A clothing card is shown behind the group issuing rations tickets. Clothing fabrics were inferior, and included synthetics made from processed wood.

AIR RAIDS A woman and child go down to a bomb shelter while (above) German civilians are helped from the wreckage of their homes.

At home, the bombing intensified. In July that year, for example, Hamburg was shattered by the first combined offensive of the British and American air forces: the USAAF bombed by day and the RAF by night, leaving more than 45,000 people dead in their wake. The Nazi Government afterwards ordered 1.2 million inhabitants to be evacuated from the flattened city, but the evacuees often failed to adapt to life in rural southern Germany where their hosts were generally unsympathetic towards the town dwellers. There was tension with farmers who were exempt from rationing: 'They eat like kings and live like pigs,' was the common complaint of evacuees.

Many children were sent from the blitzed towns to special evacuation centres where their habits of crying, bedwetting, teenage moodiness and cheekiness created as much friction with hosts as they had in Britain. As in Britain, too, there was a drift back to the towns and the life of comradeship under the bombs. People washed up together at roadside water pumps. Chains of 'rubble women' became a common sight, clearing debris from bomb-damaged buildings.

Propaganda minister Josef Goebbels was often photographed giving encouragement to survivors, but Hitler refused to visit any bombed-out towns. After Stalingrad, the Führer lived an increasingly isolated life, chiefly at his headquarters at Wolfsschanze (the wolf's lair) in a remote part of East Prussia.

His harsh voice was occasionally heard over the radio, preceded by the words *Der Führer Spricht* (The Leader Speaks), restaurants throughout the Reich were supposed to turn up their loudspeakers, and

BLOODY REPRISAL

The penalties for resistance in Nazi Germany were grim. In the most famous episode, the July Plot of 1944, a group of military officers narrowly failed in an attempt to blow up the Führer. Thousands of arrests and hundreds of executions followed. Badly shaken, Hitler had the ringleaders killed by slow hanging from butchers' hooks on nooses made from piano wire. The executions were filmed and played to the Führer, at his request.

customers to fall silent. But he was not an especially good broadcaster. The days of the mass rallies had gone – Hitler made few public speeches in wartime and did not attempt to display the magnetic powers he had once exercised as an orator.

TOTAL WAR

It was only in 1943, after defeat at Stalingrad, that the Nazi leadership belatedly tried to gear up the entire German economy for the war effort. Typically, it was Goebbels who proclaimed the policy of 'total war', in a blistering speech at Berlin's sports stadium. 'Now, nation, arise! Let the storm break loose!' he exhorted.

Under the new policy, the production of civilian goods was neglected in favour of arms manufacture. While tanks and aircraft started rolling off the assembly lines in increasing numbers, all men between 16 and 65 not in uniform were registered for compulsory labour – even criminals were put on war work – and the Hitler Youth was drafted to help out on farms. However, Nazi teaching about the woman's role in the home meant that the female workforce – so vital to the war economies of other nations – was mobilised only slowly.

The most distinctive feature of life in Germany was the enormous influx of foreign labourers. It is an irony of history that Hitler, who had dreamed of creating a 'racially pure'

LAST PHASE Berliners queue for water in the rubble of their bombed-out city. Left: only young boys and grandfathers made up the *Volkssturm* or Home Guard during the later stages of the war.

CITY OF WOMEN

At the end of the war, when the Russians launched their onslaught on Berlin, they were attacking a city of women. In March 1945, the capital's civilian population was down to 2,700,000 of whom more than 2 million were female. The males were mostly boys or veterans who were too old to serve.

Reich, ended up flooding the nation with multitudes of workers from abroad.

By 1944, over 7 million foreign men and women had been brought into Germany from the defeated nations. Civilian workers, concentration camp inmates and prisoners-of-war together made up an immense, cosmopolitan army. Forced labour was employed by electrical firms such as Siemens and Telefunken; by the motor manufacturers Daimler-Benz and BMW; by aircraft manufacturers Messerschmitt, Heinkel and Junkers; and in the colossal arms plants of Krupp.

The most despised races – Jews, Poles and Russians – were treated as slave labourers and regarded as wholly dispensable. Others were given more consideration, especially those with the valued skills of electricians, mechanics, die-makers and so on.

Conscripted labourers worked as servants in many homes. Some 500,000 Ukrainian girls were imported

to bolster numbers in domestic service, and many top
Nazis had Russian women working in their homes.

The majority, though, lived in the barrack blocks
of labour camps where, with their own canteens and
newspapers, they formed a separate society within the
Reich. German civilians had little direct contact with
them, though they were often glimpsed – a
disquieting presence – at the margin of everyday life.

Elsbeth Emmerich remembers how gas was
installed in her house: 'One day a young Polish
prisoner of war came to dig a trench outside. At
lunchtime Mum went down to him and made signs for
him to come up for something to eat. That was strictly
against the rules. No mixing with the enemy or people
from the work camps! Mum didn't take much notice of
such rules so he was soon sat at our dinner table. He
didn't say a word. He seemed frightened and very
hungry. We were also a bit frightened. What if he
decided to attack us? Of course he didn't!'

The concentration camps farmed out their inmates
to enterprises such as the I.G. Farben rubber and
chemical works (near Auschwitz), where 30,000 people
died. Fearing towards the end of the war that their
victims should fall alive into Allied hands, the SS in
Poland forced their remaining prisoners onto the
roads leading back into Germany. The emaciated
figures in their threadbare clothes were pushed along
at a hellish pace, encouraged with truncheons and
whips. Anyone who lagged behind was shot.

By now the whole fabric of social life was falling

'I FOUND A HUMAN ARM'

BREMERHAVEN, FEBRUARY 1944

❝ That evening we reached the spot where our house once stood. All we found was ashes and rubble ... The day after the bombing I heard that an enemy aircraft had been shot down and that pieces of the aircraft were scattered all over the area where our house had been. I saw the wreckage and in it a human torso, probably the pilot, burnt beyond recognition.

They said it was a British plane. I felt nothing. My own tragedy had numbed all my feelings. Later, when working in the garden, I found a human arm lying there between the dungheap and the cabbages. It was a man's arm, quite hairy, with the hand still attached. Probably what was left of one of the crew. That shocked me deeply. I reported the find to the authorities. ❞

From the recollections of Hanna Lambrecht of Langen, war bride.

apart. While the bombing of German towns reached horrific levels, refugees streaming in from the east brought with them stories of rape and other atrocities committed by the Red Army. Weariness and cynicism spread among the great queues of homeless people waiting for hot meals in the emergency kitchens set up by the army. With the daily diet below subsistence level, mobs started to pilfer stores and to derail trains for food. 'Enjoy the war – the peace will be awful', was the rueful quip on everyone's lips.

The Nazi leadership responded by intensifying their terror. While the defence of the nation was left increasingly to fanatical Hitler Youth and aged *Volkssturm* (Home Guard) members, SS teams were everywhere, shooting deserters, looters and anyone charged with defeatist talk. In Berlin, hardly a building was left intact by Allied bombs, bullets and shells. The people took to their cellars and waited in terror for the hammering of rifle butts against the cellar doors.

AFTERMATH
Allied troops help with rescue work in Berlin, 1945. Altogether, 76,652 tons of explosives and incendiaries were dropped on the city.

THE SHADOW OF FASCISM

Neither black shirts nor blustering slogans could conceal Italy's lack of enthusiasm for the

war into which the Duce led his people. When he was finally forced from power,

there was dancing in the streets.

AMONG THE MOST prominent slogans of Italian fascism were the words *'Credere! Obbedire! Combattere!'*, meaning 'Believe! Obey! Fight!' The political system was founded by Benito Mussolini and concentrated all power – in theory at least – on his person. Portraits of the jutting-jawed Duce (leader) hung in every schoolroom and civic hall, and Mussolini promoted his cult of violent action through mob oratory at rallies.

Grandiose plans for national expansion were put before the people – yet when world war came, the country was totally unprepared both economically and militarily. The Italian contribution to the Axis effort was disastrous. Defeat followed defeat in East Africa, North Africa and Greece. At home, shortages and inflation set in almost immediately, and the problems only worsened as the war went on.

The truth was that elements of sham had always lingered about the fascist regime in Italy. To begin with, Mussolini did not quite possess the absolute authority which he craved. Portraits of the King and the Pope hung alongside the Duce's in many public places, testifying to the compromises he had been forced to make with the monarchy and Church.

Certainly immense efforts were made to inculcate Fascist doctrines in schools and universities, but Italy's richer cultural traditions also endured. The liberal philosopher Benedetto Croce campaigned against the regime and, though his house was sacked by Fascist thugs, Mussolini never dared to forbid him to publish.

People bought their food from shopkeepers who supposedly were fascist, but only because they had to have a Party card or their licences were

FASCIST SALUTE Mussolini is greeted by some of his enthusiastic followers. Top right: the poster promises 'We Shall Return' (to East Africa).

taken away. Under Mussolini, many factories operated as 'corporations' – trade unions which included both employers and employees to minimise industrial strife and mobilise the whole workforce to national needs. But like so many Fascist innovations, its impact was largely superficial. A joke went the rounds about Giovanni Agnelli, the president of Fiat, who looks at his workers and complains: 'Half of them are socialists and half are Communists.' And which are the Fascists? 'Oh, all of them.'

The police – given special powers – were probably the most efficient organ of the Fascist state. They arrested thousands of opponents through the normal channels, while using plain-clothes men to subvert the efforts of thousands more. Plain-clothes officers led

the cheering at public meetings, and formed vast bodyguards when the Duce went on publicised walkabouts among his people. But the police could not stop the anti-Fascist graffiti that appeared overnight on walls as the war progressed – and they were no proof against Allied bombs.

British bombers from Mediterranean and North African bases struck regularly at Italian cities from 1940 onwards. When the United States joined the campaign, massive devastation of factories resulted. By 1943, 60 per cent of Italy's industrial production had been destroyed – overall, Italy was to lose more civilians to air attacks than blitzed Britain.

To keep up morale, Mussolini delayed rationing as long as possible; but when it came, the ration was

'MUSSOLINI IS ALWAYS RIGHT'

PROPAGANDA Mussolini used the magazine *Fascist Youth* to try to mould the minds of young Italians.

CHILDREN AT SCHOOL began every day by chanting the Fascist ten commandments, one of which ran: '*Mussolini ha sempre ragione*' ('Mussolini is always right'). In schools and universities, textbooks were revised to bring them into line with Fascist dogma. Teachers had to take an oath of loyalty to the regime while their students were indoctrinated with the fundamental idea that everything existed for the glory of the state – individual lives counted for nothing. 'Better to live one day like a lion than a hundred years as a sheep', was one of Mussolini's favourite maxims.

The comic strips in children's magazines reinforced propaganda, and youth organisations fostered fascist ideas outside school hours. At the age of four, boys had to don a little black shirt and enlist as 'Sons of the She-Wolf'. At eight, they joined a body called the *Balilla* where they marched under banners, and learned songs and salutes. Sports were encouraged too: football, boxing, swimming, athletics and shooting on miniature ranges. When they were 14, boys graduated to the

Avant-guardisti where they did formation marching with rifles, took part in mock battles and submitted to political indoctrination sessions. At eighteen, the youths entered the *Giovani fascisti avanguardisti* for a two-year course that decided whether they were suitable material for adult membership of the Fascist elite. Comparable youth groups were organised for girls. The programme of physical training and athletics for young women, however, brought Mussolini into conflict with the Catholic Church. The Vatican did not approve of such departures from womanly modesty as occurred in the hurling of javelins and mass exercises in gym clothes.

MOUNTING GUARD Italian boys at drill in the *Balilla* Musketeers.

among the lowest in all of Europe. Bread rations fell as low as 5oz (150g) per person per day. In some areas three-quarters of all farm produce found its way onto the flourishing black market. Official food distribution became a farce in which some 40 overlapping agencies came into conflict with one another, while millions of forged ration cards started to circulate among the population.

Meanwhile, the Germans' contempt for their partners' fighting ability became ever more obvious. Italians became more valued as labourers than as soldiers – at one point as many as 350,000 migrant Italian workers were toiling inside the German Reich. Humiliated beyond endurance, Mussolini began to take childish delight at news of the Germans' own military reverses at the hands of the Russians.

Cracks started to show at every level of Italian society in 1943. Despite police surveillance, workers in the factories of the north started taking strike action.

REACHING THE MASSES The front page of a Fascist party newspaper attacks the Allies. Right: Italian children pose under one of Mussolini's slogans.

The court lost all faith in Mussolini's leadership, and the King was especially alarmed by an Allied raid on Rome on July 19, 1943, in which hundreds of men, women and children were killed, and the basilica of San Lorenzo fuori le Mura was badly damaged. Repudiated even by his own party, Mussolini – the scapegoat – was stripped of some of his powers and then arrested.

THE FALL OF MUSSOLINI

When the news was announced crowds danced in the streets of Rome. A mob broke into the offices of the Fascist newspaper *Il Messagero* and threw huge portraits of the Duce out of the windows, along with the furniture and files. Fascist emblems were hacked off public buildings, and the whole edifice of Mussolini's regime collapsed in the capital with so little regret that not a single man died trying to stop the overthrow.

Shortly afterwards, though, the Germans countered by taking control of northern Italy, seizing Rome and ruling as firmly as they did in the other occupied nations of Western Europe. Rescued on Hitler's orders, Mussolini became the puppet ruler of the so-called Italian Social Republic based at Salò near Lake Garda.

The Germans, meanwhile, held the reins of power.

ROMAN SHOPFRONT Following anti-Jewish legislation, Italian shops started displaying 'Aryan' notices.

WRITING ON THE WALL 'Germany is truly your friend', a poster reassures Italians after the Nazi takeover. Right: Rome's needy crowd a soup kitchen, 1944.

In Rome orders were broadcast for all Italians to surrender their arms on pain of death. A curfew was installed, with decrees that anyone seen on the streets after five o'clock in the afternoon would be shot on sight. House arrests, street round-ups and deportations became commonplace. Jews, who had been relatively untroubled by Mussolini in his heyday, now faced the same vicious persecution in Italy as elsewhere under the Nazis.

FISH DINNERS

In the hungry days preceding the liberation of Naples, all of the tropical fish in the city's famous aquarium were eaten by inhabitants. It is said that at the banquet offered to welcome US General Mark Clark the main course was a baby manatee, the most prized item of the collection, boiled and served with garlic sauce.

General Mark Clark enters Rome, 1944.

When the Germans announced military call-up, the cities filled with young men evading service. With deserters, refugee Allied servicemen and escaped POWs swelling the numbers on the run, the country became gripped by a giant game of hide and seek.

Out of Rome's wartime population of 1.5 million, some 200,000 were being hidden by the rest, many finding refuge in churches, religious houses, rambling palaces and private apartments. In country districts, large partisan bands sprang up, encouraged by the success of Allied landings in Sicily and by news of the slow, footslogging advance up the spine of Italy.

The rural poor – peasants, shepherds, charcoal burners and others – lent assistance in their hundreds of thousands. Reprisals taken by the Germans were horrific in scale: in one instance, on March 30, 1944, 335 hostages were shot in the Ardeatine caves near Rome.

Conditions in Rome itself deteriorated rapidly during this period. Gas, electricity and water were often cut off. As in medieval times, water sellers now appeared in the streets, hawking their precious commodity to passers-by. With food prices soaring, people also swapped possessions in the streets, books, gramophone records and clothes being laid out to get money for beef, packets of salt or extra bread. In the parks, trees were felled and

'SMART NEW OVERCOATS MADE FROM CANADIAN BLANKETS'

❛ Tailors all over Naples are taking uniforms to pieces, dyeing the material, and turning them into smart new outfits for civilian wear. I hear that even British Army long-coms, which despite the climate still find their way over here, are accepted with delight, dyed red, and turned into the latest thing in track suits.

In the first days the MPs [military police] carried out a few half-hearted raids on the people specializing in these adaptations, but they found too many smart new overcoats made from Canadian blankets awaiting collection by Italian friends of General this and Colonel that to be able to put a stop to the thing. Last week the Papal Legate's car, held up by pure accident in some routine road-check, was found to be fitted with a set of stolen tyres. Many apologies and smiles and His Reverence was waved on. ❜

From the recollections of Norman Lewis, a British officer in Naples.

benches were chopped up for much-needed firewood.

In the areas liberated by the Allies, meanwhile, a black market of astonishing proportions developed. It formed the background to the famous novel *Catch-22* by Joseph Heller, then a bombardier with the United States Air Force. Every type of army equipment short of guns and ammunition was sold openly in the markets – from cigarettes and food rations to typewriters, camera film, boots, copper wire and penicillin. Army blankets, especially, were seen everywhere, adapted to make stylish women's coats and bartered in bales as a kind of currency.

In Sicily, where the Allied occupation began, corruption was especially rife due to the revival of the Mafia. One of Mussolini's few real achievements had been to suppress this secret criminal brotherhood. The Americans deliberately cultivated links with the Mafia in the fight against fascism, and its occupation regime was largely staffed by *mafiosi*.

As Italian men disappeared into battle, joining partisans in the hills or vanishing into POW camps, startling numbers of Italian girls took to prostitution. Novelist Norman Lewis, at that time a British intelligence officer, described in his diary for 1944 how romantic life in Naples was changed by the arrival of the GIs.

'An American private – who can shower cigarettes, sweets and even silk stockings in all directions – has a higher income than any Italian in Naples. The temptation is very great and few seem able to resist. Thus, the long, delicate, intricate business of the old Neapolitan courtship – as complex as the mating ritual of exotic birds – is replaced by a brutal wordless approach, and a crude act of purchase.'

Ruined Italy became a society of scavengers. With hunger gnawing at the population, thousands of women and children wandered along roadsides and into the adjoining fields to scratch for edible plants such as dandelions and plantains. Sparrows and warblers were netted for the table, and woods scoured for edible mushrooms. On beaches littered with barbed wire, people could be seen squatting round weird home-made contraptions trying to distil sea water for drinking purposes. Meanwhile, in towns devastated by bombs and shells, dance music crackled from municipal loudspeakers which had once broadcast fascist speeches. Italy under the Allied occupation was half carnival, half catastrophe.

GOODLY GRAIN
Women dry wheat amid the rubble of a ruined Italian town – one of many devastated during the liberation of Italy.

WEAPONS OF VENGEANCE

Towards the end of the war, a type of weapon never previously experienced was unleashed on London.

IT FLEW, SOMEONE remembered, 'spluttering like an ancient Ford driving uphill.' The mechanically guided, pilotless aircraft was Germany's V-1 (*Vergel-tungswaffe*, or revenge weapon), launched by a catapult 180 ft (55 m) long, with rails running along an upward curving ramp. The cement ramps were noticed by Allied aerial reconnaissance, and their appearance earned them the nickname of 'ski sites'. Meanwhile, on the ground, the resistance located over 100 of these mysterious building

DOODLING
ALONG V-1s were powered by jet propulsion. They flew straight and provided target practice for anti-aircraft batteries.

BUZZ BOMBER
V-1 flying bombs were catapulted into the air from camouflaged launch sites in northern Occupied Europe. Right: a member of the emergency services rescues a girl from her ruined home.

units. An agent named Michel Hollard, acting undercover as a modest business representative from Paris, describes how he followed up reports of the strange new construction work going on. 'The first place was Auffay, a small stop on the railway line between Rouen and Dieppe. I travelled there on the first train available – wearing clothes a workman or peasant might wear – and after leaving the station I set out to find the mysterious building sites. I walked 4

kilometres in one direction and found nothing; the second road I tried yielded no results, neither did the third, but the fourth led me straight to the heart of a building site 4 kilometres from the centre of Auffay. I found myself confronted by a veritable ant-heap of workers, bulldozers and tractors, surrounded by armed guards. The whole scene covered a site extending over approximately 400 square metres.'

The first of the V-1s crossed the Channel in June 1944, just a week after the D-Day invasion of Europe. The flying bombs arrived by day and night, chugging along like huge clockwork toys. Londoners called them 'doodlebugs' as a tribute to their weird appearance. People rapidly learned that they were safe so long as the flying bomb's engine was still emitting its buzzing noise. When the engine stopped, however, there was a harrowing silence. Everyone knew that an explosion must follow.

Later, some V-1s were launched from aircraft and, altogether, they killed more than 5000 people and injured a further 16,000, prompting a second mass evacuation of children from London. But there was one small advantage: that brief delay when they fell silent gave people a

SILENT TERROR A V-2 rocket is prepared for firing. Launched from bases in Holland, the rockets arrived in London just four minutes later, and fell to earth at up to 2500 mph (4000 km/h) with a supersonic bang. Above: one V-2 raid is reported in the Press two months after the first attack.

few seconds in which to run for cover.

In contrast, the V-2 rocket arrived without any warning whatsoever. This was the second of Hitler's revenge weapons: a ballistic missile equipped with a 1-ton warhead and fuelled by alcohol and liquid oxygen.

The Germans tested the V-2 at a top secret, well guarded artillery ground at Blizna in Poland; parts of the test missiles fired from the base fell into the surrounding forests and marshes. Although the Germans showered the area with leaflets informing residents that the explosions were caused by the dropping of 'spare fuel tanks', the Polish resistance recovered pieces of debris and had them analysed. In one of the war's most daring espionage coups, they even managed to dismantle and smuggle to London all the key parts of an entire, unexploded rocket which had buried itself in the muddy banks of the river Bug. As a result, the British authorities had some notion of what to expect before

the new wave of secret weapons was launched.

The British public, however, was taken by surprise. On September 8, 1944, just after 6pm, the London suburb of Chiswick was rocked by a terrifying explosion. Twenty houses

were destroyed by the blast, and several people killed or injured. Since there had been no sign of a doodlebug or a conventional bomber, it was thought, at first, that a gas main had exploded. It was not until November 10, 1944, that Churchill informed Parliament that the recent series of 'gas explosions' shaking entire streets resulted from V-2 attacks.

The V-2s were devastating on impact. One hit a Deptford branch of Woolworth's crowded with Saturday morning shoppers, killing 160 people, mostly women and children. Yet despite the havoc they wrought, neither of the V-weapons proved capable of altering the war's course. By the time they had come into use, the end was already in sight.

WEST END HIT A cloud of dust and rubble billows into the air as a doodlebug hits its target in central London. Many doodlebugs were shot down over south-east England, but the ones that got through caused extensive damage.

UNDER THE RISING SUN

Geishas vanished from the streets … gongs were melted down for guns …

traditional life was transformed as Japan slid from flag-waving jubilation towards

the mushroom-cloud apocalypse of Hiroshima.

PUBLIC MORALE in Japan soared sky-high with the nation's early triumphs against the Allies. In offensives as bold as Hitler's *Blitzkrieg*, Japanese troops seized Malaya, Singapore, Hong Kong and the Philippines, sweeping on through the oil-rich Dutch East Indies to threaten Australia, and pouring through Burma to the edge of the British Raj. Japan's crack soldiers were taking on white opponents – and winning – to gain control of a quarter of the globe.

Jubilant schoolboys recorded Japan's conquests with rising sun flags on wall maps. Young men called to arms were given rapturous congratulations in their neighbourhoods on receiving the draft notice, and flag-waving send-offs rang to cries of *'banzai'*, the patriotic battle cry which meant: 'May you live ten thousand years!'

Nerved up for glory, many of the young draftees

EARLY LEARNING   A Japanese schoolboy learns about aerial warfare. Below: children in Tokyo salute Japanese victories.

cared little for their personal survival. Japanese psychology placed more importance on collective pride than on individuality. And a militaristic conformism was brought to bear on the entire civilian population too. Every roof and door in Tokyo was hung with the rising sun flag. On streetcars in the capital, passengers were required to stand and bow reverently whenever the Imperial Palace came into view from the carriage.

Discipline was kept in Japan, as in other totalitarian states, by a powerful secret police. This was the feared *Kempeitai* whose red-brick-fronted headquarters in Tokyo housed a terror centre. The few whites – even Germans and Italians – resident in Japan were regarded with the utmost suspicion. After the first bombing raid on Tokyo an Anti-Espionage Week was staged, when in every Japanese city wall posters went up exhorting citizens to be vigilant. Foreigners were pursued in the streets by urchins calling out *'Spai! Spai!'* ('Spy! Spy!')

But official propaganda and the attentions of the secret police tell only part of the story. A remarkable habit

MASS SOCIETY Japanese machinists start the day by saluting the flag. Right: women workers in a munitions factory. The traditional role of women in Japanese society was revolutionised by the war.

of self-policing was already ingrained in society. Blackout drill, collecting scrap and salvage, distributing rations and so on were all done by neighbourhood associations called *tonarigumi,* who exerted strong pressure to conform.

The rationing system was particularly unusual in that there were no cards or points. Every Japanese had a right to a fixed portion of rice, but other foodstuffs were shared out at the discretion of the *tonarigumi* according to what was available. Frugal eating was already a traditional virtue in Japan. Now, with the inevitable shortages of war, the slogan was *Yase-gaman* ('Strength Through Skinniness').

Gongs, bells and metal altarpieces were taken from temples to be melted down and recast as guns. Every scrap of tinfoil was collected for use in the aircraft industry, and with such eagerness that at least one schoolchild long continued to believe that Japanese planes were actually made of silver paper. With war films playing in the movie houses and propaganda broadcasts blaring daily from the radio, enthusiasm for the war was maintained throughout 1942.

The first serious reverses in 1943, however, caused things to turn sour on the home front. The rice ration was cut, for example, to a half and then, in 1944, to a third of the normal requirement. It was also of inferior quality, adulterated with wheat, potatoes and beans. In the end, rice became virtually unobtainable and people survived on pumpkin as a staple instead. Fish – the other key element in the Japanese people's diet – was scarce.

To quell the nation's hunger pangs, every scrap of

'A CURTAIN OF LIGHT FALLING THROUGH THE AIR'

JAPAN, 1944–45

❛ I was always fascinated by the way that different people reacted to the bombing raids. Some people who were quite brave in other ways would go pale and tense when they heard the sound of the sirens, and would stumble off in a daze towards the nearest air-raid shelter. I watched many raids, particularly over Mitaka, where the Nakajima aircraft factory was situated.

At night the fire-bombing had a weird, fantastic beauty, like a curtain of light falling through the air, accompanied always by this strange sound – za-za-za – like the beating of a torrential downpour of rain. It wasn't because I was brave that I watched the raids, but because I was like my father – I didn't trust air-raid shelters. ❜

From the recollections of Lida Momo, a Japanese Communist.

'LONG, GLINTING WINGS, SHARP AS BLADES'

TOKYO, 1945

❛ The bright light dispelled the night and B-29s were visible here and there in the sky. For the first time, they flew low or middling high in staggered levels. Their long, glinting wings, sharp as blades, could be seen through the oblique columns of smoke rising from the city, suddenly reflecting the fire from the furnaces below, black silhouettes gliding through the fiery sky to reappear farther on, shining golden against the dark roof of heaven or glittering blue, like meteors, in the searchlight beams spraying the vault from horizon to horizon. There was no question in such a raid of huddling blindly underground; you could be roasted alive before you knew what was happening. All the Japanese in the gardens near mine were out of doors or peering up out of their holes, uttering cries of admiration – this was typically Japanese – at this grandiose, almost theatrical spectacle. ❜

From the recollections of Robert Guillain, resident in Tokyo at the time.

soil came under cultivation, from the tiniest window boxes to the arena of Tokyo stadium, built for the aborted 1940 Olympics. People farmed the narrow strips alongside railway tracks. In the overworked rural areas they scoured fields for grasshoppers which, boiled with soy sauce, provided protein.

Supplies of soap, matches, sandals and thread dried up. As fuel shortages began to bite, pine roots were dug up and delivered to army supervisors who took them away to be boiled into a crude fuel for warships. The armed services' needs had priority.

People shivered in their homes through lack of coal, wood and charcoal, and the traditional hot baths were no longer available.

Restaurants closed and sake (rice wine) ran out. The geisha houses were shut down on government orders and their pampered inhabitants forced to choose between war work or drifting into prostitution. Throughout Japan the exotic colours of kimonos were seen less and less as women took to wearing drab overalls.

A CHANGING SOCIETY

The role of women was transformed in Japanese society more than anywhere else. Now required to be much more than man-pleasing 'Madame Butterflies', they were obliged during the last two years of war to do compulsory service in farms and factories. 'Men to the Front – Women to the Workplace', was the slogan. By 1945 the Japanese economy relied chiefly on women and Koreans, along with prisoners of war, old people and children as young as ten.

Discipline began to crack as casualties mounted. Tsutsumi Ayako, then a schoolgirl, recalled: 'Families whose sons were killed in the war were given little plaques saying "Military Patriotic House" to hang on their gateposts. Every time we passed a house which had one of those plaques, we would stop and bow our heads in respect. But that was also something that people got more lax about as the war went on, because in the end it reached a point where you could hardly walk down the street without having to stop and bow half a dozen times.'

It was mass bombing, above all, that rocked Japan to its foundations. Though frequent air-raid drills were mounted, the authorities had made little provision for shelters. In the capital, people dug holes in their back gardens or resorted to the subway, which was too shallow to offer protection.

SAMURAI SPIRIT The poster shows the flags of the three Axis powers.
Right: sound detectors were used to warn of approaching Allied bombers.

DAZED SURVIVORS Hiroshima, ten minutes after the bomb. People did not know what had hit them.

And the level of bombing was horrific. In 1945 Tokyo was devastated by 2000 tons of incendiaries dropped by rumbling waves of 'B-san' (B-29) bombers. Ferocious firestorms swept across waterways and firebreaks. Whole families baked to death in their pitiful shelter holes, were drowned or boiled alive in the canals, or were suffocated by the phenomenal uprush of air triggered by the inferno.

Then came the ultimate horror. On Monday, August 6, 1945, a few seconds after 8.15am, a single, torpedo-shaped atomic bomb was dropped by a B-29 Superfortress flying over the city of Hiroshima. A flash of light was followed by a fireball. From the soaring pillar of smoke a mushroom cloud billowed out, moisture condensing around to fall in weirdly large black raindrops.

The whole city was practically annihilated, its buildings vaporised and much of the population left dead, dying or fleeing half-mad from the spreading fire. Some people near the epicentre of the explosion were reduced to silhouettes imprinted on concrete.

'I rubbed my nose and mouth hard with a towel I had at my waist,' a survivor recalled, 'to my horror I found that the skin of my face had come off in the towel. Oh! The skin on my hands, on my arms came off too.' Between 75,000 and 100,000 people are thought to have died in the initial explosion, while the silent, lethal radiation from the blast claimed many more victims in the months and years that followed.

On August 9 a second atomic bomb was dropped on the port and shipbuilding centre of Nagasaki. At that point, the Emperor Hirohito and his ministers decided on surrender. He is said to have announced in court Japanese: 'The war has taken a turn not necessarily to our advantage ...'

World War II was over.

IN MEMORIAM

In Tokyo, all the carnivores in the zoo were killed, on official orders, by the injection of a lethal drug. This was done to prevent the big cats and others being loosed onto the city streets after bombing. Buddhism, however, forbids the killing of animals and one of the war's strangest ceremonies was a memorial service for the zoo animals, held in the capital, where the scientists responsible asked forgiveness from the spirits of their victims.

IT'S OVER!

'Ah, it was a sea of people', General de Gaulle wrote of his triumphant parade

down the Champs Elysées in August 1944. And, with victory assured, waves of rejoicing

humanity engulfed Allied capitals all over the world.

ON SATURDAY August 26, 1944, General de Gaulle made his official entry into his liberated capital, Paris. The Nazi swastika had been removed from the Eiffel Tower and a vast tricolour hung from it instead. Four tanks led the parade as the tall, unmistakable figure of the General made his way down the Champs Elysées at the head of a group of Resistance leaders. Paris was in a mood to celebrate, despite the fact that isolated bursts of shooting could still be heard in various parts of the city as the Free French forces continued to round up fugitive Germans and collaborators.

Long before the war ended formally in Europe, celebrations were held in a number of liberated capitals. Rejoicing was often marred by ugly scenes as reprisals were taken against collaborators; girls who had gone out with Germans were particular targets, often having their heads shaved and being paraded in shame through the streets. But the war went on, and it was not until the small hours of the morning of May 7, 1945, that Germany acknowledged defeat as General Alfred Jodl signed an unconditional surrender. Hitler was already dead – he had committed suicide a week earlier in his Berlin bunker. And soon after hearing of the surrender, Churchill and the new US president Harry S Truman agreed that the following day, May 8, should be celebrated as Victory in Europe (VE) Day.

In Britain, families heard the BBC confirm the news. It was drizzling lightly in London as VE Day dawned, but the grey skies could not prevent elated crowds from streaming into the capital's streets from an early hour. At three o'clock Churchill broadcast to the nation, proceeding afterwards from Downing Street to the House of Commons in a car pushed along Whitehall by the pressure of the cheering multitudes. That night the street lights were switched on all over Britain for the first time since the war's outbreak. For children who had grown up under the blackout it was like a fairyland. London's rejoicing crowds flocked around Buckingham Palace where King George VI let the Princesses Elizabeth and Margaret mingle unnoticed with the revellers outside. 'Poor darlings,' he wrote in his diary, 'they have never had any fun yet.' A massive hokey-cokey surrounded Queen Victoria's statue and uniformed servicemen were carried shoulder-high through Piccadilly.

Moscow, Paris, Copenhagen, The Hague ... all erupted in similar fashion. In Moscow, at the victory parade, captured Nazi standards were piled at the feet of Soviet leaders in Red Square. At Halifax in Canada things got out of hand as thousands of drunken sailors went on a rampage, looting shops and sometimes setting fire to premises. In

PARIS PARADE French freedom fighters rejoice at the liberation of Paris, August 1944.

AMERICAN CELEBRATIONS New Yorkers glory in the coming of VE Day.

LONDON AND MOSCOW   Britons cheer Winston Churchill after his announcement of Victory in Europe on May 8, 1945. Top: crowds celebrate in the Russian capital.

the United States, too, there were celebrations, but the war with Japan still loomed large in everyone's mind. It was two and a half months later, when the Japanese surrendered, that America went on its great spree.

Victory over Japan (VJ) Day was August 15. In Washington DC, White House guards could not keep delirious crowds from surging onto the lawn. The heart of New York City became a human ocean as over a million revellers descended on the Times Square area. The vast, spontaneous shenanigans covered the length of the country: as far north as Barrow in Alaska a band of Eskimos was reported victory-dancing to the music of drums made of walrus hides stretched across driftwood hoops. Australia, like the United States, had waited with special keenness for the Japanese surrender. Now, as the cheering multitudes filled Sydney's streets, office workers showered down a swirling blizzard of ticker-tape – improvised from shredded income-tax forms.

For the defeated nations, things were different. In Germany the hunting down of war criminals was underway, with an intensive denazification programme to rid society of Party loyalists. In some areas, disbelieving civilians were forced to watch documentary films of what had gone on in the concentration camps. Everywhere, war-weary veterans and refugees haunted the rubble of ruined cities. Women queued outside Allied billets for scraps discarded by servicemen – they cooked on open fires in their half-demolished homes and washed their threadbare sheets on the riverbanks. A 'cigarette economy' emerged, the cigarette serving as the basic unit of exchange for everything from a Leica camera to the services of a prostitute.

Italy was also in chaos. Mussolini and his mistress, Clara Petacci, had been shot by partisans and strung up by their heels for display in Milan's Piazza Loretto. Famine was rife, inflation reached incredible heights and bandits roamed country areas in gangs formed from groups of deserters, armed with the weapons that littered fields and hedgerows. In Tokyo, crowds wept before the Imperial palace. The city was now a wasteland of charred wood and pulverised brick, where thousands of homeless people squatted in makeshift shelters.

Despite the massive American aid that came after the war, austerity long permeated civilian life across the face of the battered planet.

TEARFUL REUNION Two freed prisoners of war embrace in Paris.

TIME CHART

NEWS OF THE WORLD

Sept 1 Germany invades Poland.

Sept 3 Britain, France, Australia and New Zealand declare war on Germany.

Sept 10 Canada declares war on Germany and the British Expeditionary Force enters France.

Sept 17 Soviet troops invade Poland and, after Warsaw falls to the Germans, Poland is effectively partitioned between Germany and the Soviet Union.

1940
Apr 9 Germany invades Norway and Denmark in a renewed *blitzkrieg* that ends the so-called Phoney War.

May 10 Germany invades Holland, Luxembourg, Belgium and France.

MARCHE DE TRIOMPHE German troops march into Paris, June 1940.

May 10 Winston Churchill replaces Neville Chamberlain as Prime Minister in Britain.

May 26 Britain begins to evacuate troops from Dunkirk.

June 10 Italy declares war on France and Britain.

June 14 Paris falls to the Germans.

June 22 France concludes armistice with Germany, signed in the same railway coach that witnessed the surrender of Germany in 1918.

Sept 3 The USA agrees to send 50 destroyers to Britain in exchange for leased bases in Newfoundland and the Caribbean.

Sept 7 The London Blitz begins.

LEISURE AND LEARNING

Sept 12 Britain sets up ENSA, the Entertainments National Service Association, to entertain troops and war workers at home and overseas.

1940
May 15 The first nylon stockings go on sale in the USA.

Sept 12 Four boys discover paintings that turn out to be some 15,000 years old on

FRANKLY MY DEAR Gable and Leigh star in *Gone With the Wind.*

the walls of a cave at Lascaux in south-west France.

Dec 25 Rodgers and Hart's *Pal Joey* opens on Broadway, with Gene Kelly and Vivienne Segal.

FILMS *Gone With the Wind* starring Clark Gable and Vivien Leigh; *The Wizard of Oz* starring Judy Garland. **1940** *The Great Dictator*, directed by and starring Charlie Chaplin; Walt Disney's *Fantasia.*

HIT SONGS *Moonlight Serenade* by Glenn Miller; and a couple of morale-boosting war songs – *There'll Always Be An England* and *Hang Out the Washing on the Siegfried Line.* **1940** *You Are My Sunshine* by James Houston Davis and Charles Mitchell; *A Nightingale Sang in Berkeley Square.*

BOOKS *Finnegans Wake* by James Joyce; *How Green Was My Valley* by Richard Llewellyn; *The Grapes of Wrath* by John Steinbeck. **1940** *Darkness at Noon* by Arthur Koestler; *For Whom the Bell Tolls* by Ernest Hemingway; *Farewell, My Lovely* by Raymond Chandler.

LIQUID SOLUTION Before nylon stockings appeared, women 'painted' their legs.

SAVE ON STOCKINGS
Silktona
LIQUID SILK STOCKINGS

LIFESTYLE CHANGES

Sept 1 Hitler's Reich decrees that listening to foreign radio broadcasts is punishable by penal servitude or, in certain cases, death.

Blackouts begin in Britain; air-raid sirens are sounded for the first time, and women and children are evacuated from cities.

Sept 23 Petrol rationing begins in Britain.

Oct 4 The 'Dig for Victory' campaign is launched in Britain, encouraging people to grow their own food.

Nov 16 Clothes rationing begins in Germany.

1940
Jan 8 Britain rations butter, sugar, bacon and ham.

Jan 15 Germany bans people from taking baths (except on Saturday and Sunday) in order to save fuel.

Feb 6 Britain launches an anti-gossip campaign:

with slogans such as 'Careless talk costs lives'.

May 14 Japan, already at war with China, rations sugar and matches.

May 30 The British government orders the removal of signposts and street names.

July 13 To stop German propagandists spreading disinformation, BBC newsreaders begin announcing their identities at the start of each broadcast: 'This is the one o'clock news, and this is Frank Phillips reading it.'

Oct 17 London Transport starts calling in country buses for use in the capital since so many of London's red double-deckers have been destroyed in the Blitz.

COUPON CULTURE Petrol **rationing is introduced in Britain.**

1941

NEWS OF THE WORLD

DEVASTATION Bomb damage in London during the Blitz.

Apr 6 Germany invades Yugoslavia and Greece.

May 10 Rudolf Hess, Hitler's Deputy Führer, is arrested on a mysterious secret mission in Scotland.

June 22 Germany invades Russia under Operation Barbarossa.

July 3 In a broadcast to Soviet people, Stalin calls for a scorched-earth policy: 'Blow up roads and bridges, wreck telephone and telegraph lines, set fire to forest, stores and transport.'

Aug 11 Winston Churchill and F.D. Roosevelt sign the Atlantic Charter, which contains eight articles of agreement between Britain and the USA over war aims.

Sept 3 The Nazis use gas chambers for the first time, killing Soviet POWs at Auschwitz.

Oct 20 Germany begins the siege of Moscow.

Dec 7 Japan bombs the US base at Pearl Harbor on the Hawaiian island of Oahu, sinking five battleships, destroying 200 aircraft, severely damaging a number of cruisers and destroyers, and killing almost 2500 men.

Dec 8 The USA and Britain declare war on Japan, Roosevelt speaking of 'a date which will live in infamy'.

Dec 11 Germany and Italy declare war on the USA.

LEISURE AND LEARNING

Jan 23 Gertrude Lawrence and Danny Kaye star in *Lady in the Dark*, with music by Kurt Weill and lyrics by Ira Gershwin.

Apr 28 The first daily drama serial, *Front-Line Family*, is broadcast by the BBC Overseas Service.

June 1 CBS transmits the first experimental colour television service from New York.

July 1 The first commercial television station, NBC's WNBT New York, broadcasts its first advertisement: a Bulova clock.

FILMS Orson Welles directs and stars in *Citizen Kane*; producer-directors Michael Powell and Emeric Pressburger release *Forty-Ninth Parallel*, a propaganda tale about Nazis on the run.

HIT SONGS *(There'll Be Bluebirds Over) the White Cliffs of Dover* by Nat Burton and Walter Kent; *Chattanooga Choo Choo* by Harry Warren; *Deep in the Heart of Texas* by Don and June Hershey Swander; *Boogie-Woogie Bugle Boy* by Don Raye and Hughie Prince.

BOOK *The Last Tycoon* by Scott Fitzgerald.

CHART TOPPER *The White Cliffs of Dover* hits the top. Left: Orson Welles in *Citizen Kane*.

LIFESTYLE CHANGES

Jan 23 An order issued in occupied France makes it illegal to 'discard, burn, or destroy, except for reasons of public health, metal scrap, old paper, feathers, rubber, bones, hides, or hair'.

Feb 12 A British policeman suffering from blood poisoning becomes the world's first recipient of penicillin, the antibiotic derived from an everyday fungus, at the Radcliffe Infirmary, Oxford. Despite the treatment, he subsequently died.

May 3 A patient with an enormous carbuncle is successfully treated with penicillin at the Radcliffe Infirmary, Oxford, opening the way for the commercial production of the antibiotic. As a result, countless lives will be saved both during the war and after it.

June 2 Britain rations clothes.

July 1 Coal restrictions begin in Britain.

Sept 1 The Nazi government in Germany orders all Jews to wear the Star of David.

Nov 1 Food rationing is introduced throughout Russia.

CRIMINAL RECORD Jews faced fines or imprisonment for not wearing the Star of David.

MEDALS FOR MOTHERS Awarded to mothers who had more than four children.

1942

OVER HERE American GIs fill the streets of London on their way to fight in Europe.

Jan 26 The first American GIs arrive in Britain.

Feb 15 Singapore falls to the Japanese.

Mar 14 American GIs arrive in Australia.

May 2 The Japanese take Mandalay; Burma is now entirely under their control.

Aug 22 The Germans launch their assault on Stalingrad.

Sept 8 The Germans reach Stalingrad.

Nov 4 Montgomery leads the British to victory over Rommel at El Alamein, forcing Axis troops to retreat from North Africa.

Nov 8 Operation Torch gets underway as Eisenhower leads the Allied landings in Morocco and Algeria.

Dec 2 Physicists Enrico Fermi, Leo Szilard, and Edward Teller successfully produce the first-ever controlled, self-sustaining nuclear chain reaction, in a squash court at the University of Chicago's Stagg Field.

Dec 24 The first surface-to-surface guided missile is launched at Peenemunde on the Baltic.

Jan 24 Entrepreneur Mike Todd brings *Star and Garter* to the Music Box Theater on Broadway, with Gypsy Rose Lee, Bobby Clark and Georgia Sothern.

Feb 10 Glenn Miller is presented with the world's first golden disc for selling a million copies of *Chattanooga Choo Choo*.

Nov 2 *Stars and Stripes*, a daily paper for American GIs in Europe, begins publication.

FILMS Michael Curtiz directs *Casablanca*, starring Humphrey Bogart and Ingrid Bergman, with Dooley Wilson singing the immortal *As Time Goes By*; Walt Disney releases *Bambi*; Greer Garson stars in *Mrs Miniver*, Hollywood's version of English life during the Blitz; Noel Coward produces, co-directs with David Lean, writes the script and score of *In Which We Serve*, a powerful propaganda film about the sinking of a British naval destroyer.

HIT SONGS *White Christmas* is written by Irving Berlin; sung by Bing Crosby, it would, by 1965, have sold a record-breaking 25 million copies. *Praise The Lord And Pass The Ammunition* is written by Frank Loesser after a remark said to have been uttered by a US Navy chaplain during Pearl Harbor. *The White Cliffs of Dover,* sung by Vera Lynn, reminds the British troops of home.

BOOKS *Go Down, Moses* by William Faulkner; *The Stranger* by Albert Camus; *Dragon's Teeth* by Upton Sinclair; *The Moon is Down* by John Steinbeck; *Put out More Flags* by Evelyn Waugh.

STIFF UPPER LIP Noel Coward plays the archetypal British officer in *In Which We Serve*.

Mar 31 Ration books for sugar and other food supplies are distributed across the USA.

Apr 6 Germany rations potatoes.

May 15 The USA rations gasoline.

May 29 Parisian Jews are forced to wear the yellow Star of David.

June 5 The Cooperative Society of Romford launches Britain's first self-service grocery store, a forerunner of the first British supermarket at Manor Park (1948).

June 6 The first jump using a parachute made of nylon takes place over Hertford, England.

Oct Oxfam founded by Gilbert Murray.

Nov 29 Coffee is rationed in the USA.

Dec 1 Economist William Beveridge produces his 'Report on Social Security' which provides a blueprint for the welfare state.

VICTORY GARDENS With food rationed, production is vital, and these American students set off to work in their college garden.

1943

NEWS OF THE WORLD

UNDER SIEGE Russian soldiers battle for Stalingrad.

Jan 31 The Battle of Stalingrad ends in surrender by the Germans; this concludes a five-month offensive that claimed the lives of 750,000 Russians and 400,000 Germans.

Apr 19 German troops attack the 500,000 Polish Jews crammed into a ghetto in Warsaw; many Jews are either killed then or will later be exterminated in concentration camps.

May 17 The RAF's 617 squadron, later known as The Dambusters, completes its mission to destroy the Mohne and Eder dams, using 'bouncing' bombs developed by Dr Barnes Wallis.

July 10 An airborne force of British and American and Canadian troops launch the Allied invasion of Sicily.

July 25 Mussolini is overthrown in Italy and Marshal Pietro Badoglio forms a new government.

Aug 27 The German Luftwaffe launches its Hs 293, the first air-to-surface guided missile, in a successful attack on HMS *Egret* in the Bay of Biscay.

Sept 3 Italy surrenders to the Allies.

Oct 13 Italy declares war on Germany.

Nov 28 Teheran hosts the first summit attended by Churchill, Roosevelt and Stalin; the agenda includes an Allied landing in France.

LEISURE AND LEARNING

Mar 31 Rodgers and Hammerstein's *Oklahoma!* opens at the St James Theater on Broadway.

June 1 British actor Leslie Howard dies. He was in a plane shot down by the Germans over the Bay of Biscay on its way from Lisbon to Bristol. He will be remembered for playing parts such as Ashley Wilkes in *Gone With the Wind*.

July 19 An Allied bombing raid on Rome avoids most of the ancient sites and buildings.

FILMS Orson Welles and Joan Fontaine star in Charlotte Bronte's *Jane Eyre*; Joseph Cotten and Teresa Wright star in Alfred Hitchcock's thriller *Shadow of a Doubt*; Gary Cooper and Ingrid Bergman star in *For Whom the Bell Tolls*, based on Ernest Hemingway's novel.

HIT SONGS *You'll Never Know* by Dick Haymes and the Song Spinners; *All Or Nothing At All* by Frank Sinatra; *My Heart and I*; *I'll Be Seeing You*; *Oh, What a Beautiful Morning*.

BOOKS *Arrival and Departure* by Arthur Koestler; *The Little Prince* by Saint-Exupery; *Caught* by Henry Green; *Ministry of Fear* by Graham Greene; *Wide is the Gate* by Upton Sinclair.

MATINEE IDOLS Gary Cooper and Ingrid Bergman in *For Whom the Bell Tolls*.

LIFESTYLE CHANGES

CLOTHES WAR Utility fashions and homemade clothes are the order of the day.

Feb 18 As part of Germany's new 'Total War' policy, sweetshops, luxury restaurants and nightclubs are closed; professional sport is stopped; and fashion magazines are banned.

May 3 Part-time work becomes compulsory for all women in Britain between the ages of 18 and 45.

May 10 Rosamond Gilmour from Croydon, Surrey, becomes Britain's first air hostess on a BOAC shuttle-service

REFUGEES Mother and child wait for a new home.

flight from Whitchurch, Somerset, to Shannon in the Irish Republic.

June 10 The Hungarian hypnotist and journalist Lazlo Biro patents the first ballpoint pen, to be manufactured the following year.

June 18 Britain's General Post Office (GPO) introduces the first prestamped aerogramme for Forces Mail.

Aug 1 Germany suspends the issue of clothing coupons, and the government calls for the evacuation of women, children and pensioners from Berlin.

Dec 2 The first Bevin Boys, drawn from young men called up for the Armed Forces, go down British mines.

1944

Mar 18 German troops enter Hungary.

June 4 The Allies enter Rome and are greeted by cheering crowds. Roosevelt comments: 'The first Axis capital is in our hands. One up and two to go.'

June 6 D-Day. Under the overall command of General Eisenhower, 5000 ships cross the English Channel and launch more than 150,000 men on to the shores of Normandy in France.

June 13 The first V-1 flying bomb hits Britain.

July 3 The Russians recapture Minsk and take 100,000 Germans prisoner.

FREE AT LAST
General de Gaulle in the streets of Paris on August 26, the day after it was liberated.

June 19 The Battle of the Philippine Sea ends with more than 300 Japanese aircraft lost compared to only 27 US planes.

July 20 Some of Hitler's generals and other officers attempt to assassinate him; although the bomb explodes, the July Plot fails and Hitler is unharmed.

Aug 25 General de Gaulle enters Paris.

Sept 3 Brussels is liberated from the Germans.

Sept 8 The first liquid-fuelled V-2 rockets fall on London – in all, over 1000 will fall on Britain, killing some 2700 people and injuring many others.

Nov 29 The first night raid on Tokyo by American B-29s.

SILENT DEATH
A V-2 rocket on its way to England.

Jan 28 Cole Porter's *Mexican Hayride* opens at the Winter Garden Theater on Broadway.

Dec 16 Glenn Miller's plane is reported missing on a routine flight to France.

Dec English Decca releases the first high-fidelity (hi-fi) recordings.

ESCAPISM **One of the year's hit films, with the ever-popular Judy Garland.**

FILMS Laurence Olivier directs and stars in Shakespeare's *Henry V*; Billy Wilder directs Edward G. Robinson, Fred McMurray and Barbara Stanwyck in the crime thriller *Double Indemnity*; Vincente Minelli directs Judy Garland, Margaret O'Brien, Leon Ames and Mary Astor in *Meet Me In St Louis*, a tale about a middle-class family at the turn of the 20th century.

HIT SONGS *Don't Fence Me In* by Bing Crosby with the Andrews Sisters and the Vic Schoen orchestra; *Rum and Limonada* by the Andrews Sisters with the Vic Schoen

orchestra; *Into Each Life Some Rain Must Fall* by Ella Fitzgerald and the Inkspots; *You Always Hurt The One You Love* by the Mills Brothers.

BOOKS *Fair Stood the Wind For France* by H.E. Bates; *Four Quartets* by T.S. Eliot; *The Razor's Edge* by Somerset Maugham.

D-DAY LANDINGS **Allied troops struggle onto the beaches of Normandy after overcoming fierce resistance.**

Apr 6 Britain introduces the PAYE (pay-as-you-earn) system of income tax.

July Preparing for the economic problems that would face the Western world after the war, the United Nations Monetary and Financial Conference held at Bretton Woods, New Hampshire, USA, endorses moves to set up the World Bank and the International Monetary Fund.

Aug 3 The British Parliament passes an Education Act which provides all children with a free secondary education.

Aug 12 Germany introduces post and railway restrictions.

Sept 1 Theatres, opera houses and music halls close down in Germany.

Sept 17 A partial 'dim-out' replaces the blackout in Britain.

Nov 9 Blue babies can lead normal lives after Alfred Blalock successfully operates on a child's heart at Johns Hopkins Children's Hospital, USA.

1945

NEWS OF THE WORLD

Jan 17 Soviet troops take Warsaw.

Jan 26 Auschwitz liberated by the Red Army.

Mar 18 Japanese schools and universities are shut down as everyone over the age of six is mobilised for the war effort.

Mar 22 The League of Arab States is formed, bringing together Egypt, Saudi Arabia, Syria, Lebanon, Jordan and the Yemen.

Apr 12 Roosevelt dies and is replaced by Harry S Truman as President of the USA.

Apr 28 Italian partisans execute Mussolini.

Apr 30 Hitler commits suicide in Berlin.

May 7 Germany surrenders.

May 8 The victorious nations celebrate VE Day.

June 26 The United Nations Charter is signed in San Francisco.

July 5 Britain holds a General Election. Churchill loses and is replaced by the Labour Party's Clement Attlee.

Aug 6 The USA drops the first atomic bomb on Hiroshima, killing 75,000 Japanese civilians immediately and a similar number soon afterwards from burns and radiation sickness.

Aug 9 The USA drops a second atomic bomb (codename 'Big Boy') on Nagasaki, killing some 65,000 Japanese civilians and a similar number soon afterwards from burns and radiation sickness.

Aug 15 World War II ends as the Japanese surrender.

DANCING FOR JOY Celebrating victory, New York style.

LEISURE AND LEARNING

VICTORY A Soviet magazine celebrates the end of the war. Above right: cinema audiences are spellbound by Gregory Peck and Ingrid Bergman.

Apr 18 The Berlin Philharmonic Orchestra gives its last concert of the war: Wagner's *Die Götterdämmerung* (The Twilight of the Gods).

Apr 19 Rodgers and Hammerstein's

Carousel opens at New York's Majestic Theater, with John Raitt as Billy Bigelow and Jan Clayton as Julie Jordan.

FILMS Alfred Hitchcock directs Gregory Peck and Ingrid Bergman in the psychological thriller *Spellbound,* from a story by Francis Beeding and with a dream sequence designed by Salvador Dali; William Wellman directs Burgess Meredith and Robert Mitchum in *The Story of GI Joe.*

HIT SONGS *Sentimental Journey* by Doris Day and the Les Brown orchestra; *Till The End Of Time* by Perry Como and the Roger Case orchestra.

BOOKS *Animal Farm* by George Orwell; *The Age of Reason* by Jean-Paul Sartre; *Brideshead Revisited* by Evelyn Waugh; *Cannery Row* by John Steinbeck.

LIFESTYLE CHANGES

A HELPING HAND A British mother collects her Family Allowance.

Jan 25 The world's first fluoridated water supply comes on stream at Grand Rapids, Michigan.

June 15 Britain introduces Family Allowances – 5 shillings for every child after the first.

July 30 The first daily

WEIGHTY WORDS The French philosopher Jean-Paul Sartre publishes *The Age of Reason.*

drama serial to be broadcast to listeners in Britain is the BBC Light Programme's *The Robinson Family.*

Oct 2 Fluorescent lighting comes to Britain: installed on a platform at Piccadilly Circus Underground station.

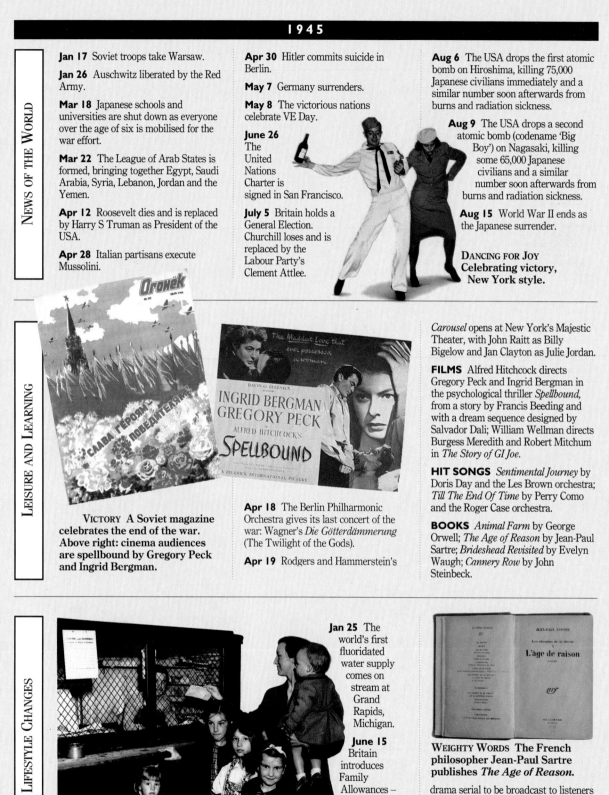

INDEX

Acknowledgments

Abbreviations
T = Top; M = Middle; B = Bottom; R = Right; L=Left.

1 Bettmann Archive. 2-3 Popperfoto. 4 Imperial War Museum Department of Art, TL; David King, TM, TR, BL; Jean-Loup Charmet, TR; Arthur Lockwood, M. 5 The Advertising Archives, TR; Bettmann Archive, M; Jean-Loup Charmet, BL; Colorific, BM, BR. 6 Ullstein Bilderdienst, BL; Robert Hunt, BR.7 Imperial War Museum, Dept of Photography. 8 Popperfoto. 9 Novosti Press. 10 Library of Congress. 11 Robert Hunt Library. 12 Imperial War Museum, Dept of Photography, BL, BR. 13 Hulton-Deutsch, TL; The John Frost Library, TR; Imperial War Museum, Dept of Photography, B. 14 Imperial War Museum, Dept of Art, TR, BL; Hulton-Deutsch, M. 15 Imperial War Museum, Dept of Photography, BL, BR. 16 Imperial War Museum, Dept of Art, TL; Hulton-Deutsch, TR; 18 Private Collection. 19 Hulton-Deutsch, T; John Frost, TR; Illustration by Peter Morter, BL; 20 Camera Press, Photo Bill Brandt. 21 Imperial War Museum, Dept of Photography, TL; Imperial War Museum, Dept of Art, MR. 22-23 Illustration by Mel Wright. 24 Robert Opie Collection, BL; Syndication International, BR. 25 Imperial War Museum, Dept of Photography; Robert Opie Collection, BR. 26 Imperial War Museum, Dept of Art, TR; Camera Press, BR. 27 Hulton-Deutsch, BL; Imperial War Museum, Dept of Art, BR. 28 Photography, Norman Brand (IWM, Dept of Exhibits & Firearms), TR, ML; Christine Vincent, MR; Private Collection, BL; John Frost, BR. 29 Christine Vincent, TL, BR; Photography, Norman Brand (IWM, Dept of Exhibits & Firearms) TM, TR, BL, BM; Jonathan Croall, TR. 30 Robert Opie Collection, BL; Hulton-Deutsch, BR. 31 Imperial War Museum, Dept of Photography, TL; Robert Opie Collection, TR. 32 Robert Opie Collection, TL; Syndication International, B. 33 Hulton-Deutsch, T, B. Jean-Loup Charmet, TL; The Granger Collection, TM; Martin Breese/Retrograph Archive, TR; Popperfoto, BL; Bettmann Archive/UPI, BR. 35 Imperial War Museum, Dept of Printed Books, TL; Private Collection, TM; Jean-Loup Charmet, TR; Bettmann Archive/UPI, BR. 36 Hulton-Deutsch, BL; Robert Reynolds, BR. 37 448TH Group Collection, Norwich, BL; Robert Opie Collection, BL; Hulton Deutsch, BR. 38 Imperial War Museum, Dept of Art, TL; Imperial War Museum, Dept of Photography, B. 39 Jersey Evening Post, TL, TR. 40 The Robert Hunt Library, TR. 40-41 Photography by Norman Brand (IWM, Dept of Exhibits & Firearms). 42 Jean Stafford. 43 Imperial War Museum, Dept of Photography, L; Popperfoto, TR. 44 The Advertising Archives. 45 Hulton-Deutsch, TL, TR; Syndication International, BL. 46 Roger-Viollet, TR; Hulton-Deutsch, BL. 47 Hulton-Deutsch, TR; Topham Picture Library, M; The Kobal Collection, TR; Imperial War Museum, Dept of Document, ML; From World War Two Through German Eyes by James Lucas Arms & Armour press, MR; Imperial War Museum, Dept of Photography, BL; Farabola, Milan,

BR. 48 Imperial War Museum, Dept of Photography, BL, BR. 49 Local History Collection, Durban, TL, TR. 50 National Archives, TL; Imperial War Museum, Dept of Photography, TR. 51 Culver Pictures Inc. 52 Culver Pictures Inc, BL. 53 Imperial War Museum, Dept of Art. 54 The Advertising Archives, MR, BL. 55 The Granger Collection, TL; The Advertising Archives, TR 56 Imperial War Museum, Dept of Art, TL; Bettmann Archive, TM; The Granger Collection, TR; Culver Pictures Inc, B 57 Bettmann Archive. 58 Bettmann Archive, BL; The Granger Collection, BR. 59 Bettmann Archive, TR, BR; Hulton-Deutsch, TL; Culver Pictures Inc, BL, BM. 60 Bettmann Archive, BL; The Granger Collection, BR. 61 Bettmann Archive, TL, BL; Culver Pictures Inc, TR. 62 National Archives, TL; Bettmann Archive, TR. 63 Bettmann Archive, TL; Culver Pictures Inc, TR. 64 Bettmann Archive 65 Library of Congress/Bettmann Archive B 66 Retrograph Archive, TL, TR, BM; Pictorial Press, BL; The Advertising Archives, BR. 67 Pictorial Press, TL; Photograhy by Norman Brand (Retrograph Archives), BL; Rex Features, BR. 68 Syndication International, BL; The Kobal Collection, BR. 69 Bettmann Archive T, B 68-69 The Kobal Collection. 70 Bettmann Archive, T. 71 The Kobal Collection, TR. 70-71 Culver Pictures Inc, B. 72 The Granger Collection, TL; Bettmann Archive, TR; Culver Pictures Inc, B. 73 Bettmann Archive, TL; BFI, TR. 74 BFI, BL; The Kobal Collection, BR. 75 Bettmann Archive, TL, TR, BL. 70 Jean-Loup Charmet, BL; Hulton-Deutsch, BR. 76 The Advertising Archives, TL; Roger-Viollet, TR. 77 Imperial War Museum, Dept of Art, BL, BR; Bettmann Archive, BM. 78 Bettmann Archive, T, BL, BR; Library of Congress, BR. 79 Bettmann Archive, TL, B; Imperial War Museum, Dept of Art, TR; Bettmann Archive, B. 80 Robert Opie Collection, T; Jean-Loup Chramet, M; Bettmann Archives/UPI, B. 81 Advertisement from Le Soir: © Hergé/Casterman, from *Tintin and The World of Hergé*, edited by Benoît Peeters, TL; Vintage Magazine Company, © D. C. Comics, TM, TR, *The Beano*, © April 12, 1941 D. C. Thomson; *The Hotspur*, © March 25, 1944, BL; Hulton-Deutsch B. 82 Bettmann Archive, T; Culver Pictures Inc, B. 83 Bettmann Archive. 84 Bettmann Archive. 85 Jean-Loup Charmet, BL; 86 The Robert Hunt Library, BR. 87 The Robert Hunt Library. 88 Roger Viollet, BL, BR. 89 The Robert Hunt Library, T; Roger-Viollet, BL; Jean -Loup Charmet, BR. 90 Martin Breese/Retrograph Archives, TL, TM, TR; Bettmann Archive. 91 Martin Breese/Retrograph Archives, TL, ML, BR; Roger- Viollet, TM; Popperfoto, TR; Bettmann Archive/UPI, BL. 92 Roger- Viollet, BL, BR. 93 Roger-Viollet, TL, M. 94 Bettmann Archive. 95 Roger-Viollet, ML; From Dat Kan Ons Niet Gebeuren by Evert Werkman, Madelon de Keizer & Gert Van Setten: De Bezige Bij, Amsterdam, 1980, BR. 94-95 Bettmann Archive. 96 Bettmann Archive, BL; From Dat Kan Ons Niet Gebeuren by Evert Werkman, Madelon de Keizer & Gert Van Setten: De Bezige Bij, Amsterdam, 1980. 97 Jean-Loup

Charmet. 98-99 Roger-Viollet. 98 Roger Viollet, B. 99 Jean-Loup Charmet, T; Rijksinstituut Voor Oorlogsdocumentaleig, B. 100 Bettmann Archive; The Advertising Archives, BR. 101 Topham Picture Library, TL; S & G Press Agency Ltd, TR; Robert Hunt Library, BL; Imperial War Museum, Dept of Documents, BM; Ullstein Bilderdienst, BR. 102 Roger-Viollet, BL, Jean-Loup Charmet, BR. 103 Roger-Viollet, BL. 104 Roger-Viollet, TL, TR; Imperial War Museum, Dept of Art, ML. 105 The Granger collections, TR; Camera Press, B. 106 Philips Eindhoven, Bureau Archiefzaken, M; Cas Oorthuys Archives, Amsterdam, BL; Rigmor Delphin, BR. 107 Roger-Viollet, TR; Robert Hunt Library, BL. 108 Cartoon by David Low © *Evening Standard*, John Frost Library, TL; The Granger Collection, Garvens from *Kladderadatsch*, MR; Colonel Blimp by David Low, © *London Evening Standard*, E.T. Archive, BR. 109 George Baker, © *Yank*, Vintage Magazine Company, TL; *Jane*, by W. Norman Pett © Mirror Group Newspapers John Frost Archive, TM; Jean-Loup Charmet, TR; Daniel R. FitzPatrick, © St. Louis Post-Dispatch; The Granger Collection, ML; Adolf Hitler by Zec, © Mirror Group Newspapers, Private Collection, BR. 110 Roger-Viollet, T, MR; Jean-Loup Charmet, BL. 111 David King Collection. 113 David King Collection, T, R. 114 David King Collection, TL, TM, TR, BR. 115 Sovfoto, BM, BR. 116 Sovfoto, TR; David King Collection, TR. 117 Camera Press. 118 David King Collection. 119 Camera Press, T; From Menschen In Ghetto by Gunther Deschner, Berielsmann Sachbuchverlag 1969, B. 120 Camera Press, BL, BM, BR. 121 Hulton-Deutsch. 123 Ullstein Bilderdienst, TL; Poster by Ludwig Hohlwein, TR; Imperial War Museum, Dept of Printed Books, ML. 124 Ullstein Bilderdienst, BL; Photography Norman Brand, (Imperial War Museum, Dept of Exhibits & Firearms), BL, BR. 125 Bettmann Archive, TL; The Advertising Archive, TR; Bettmann Archive, BL, BR. 126 Private Collection, BL; Ullstein Bilderdienst, BM, BR. 127 Ullstein Bilderdienst, TL; Imperial War Museum, Dept of Art; TR; From Menschen In Ghetto by Gunther Deschner, B. 128 Ullstein Bilderdienst. 129 Wiener Library, T; Private Collection, BL. 130 Private Collection, TL; Bundesarchiv, TR, BR. 131 Robert Hunt Library. 132 Robert Hunt Library, BL, BR. 133 Ullstein Bilderdienst, TL; Bettmann Archive, TR. 134 Ullstein Bilderdienst, BR; Sovfoto, BR. 135 Imperial War Museum, Dept of Photography. 136 Imperial War Museum, Dept of Photography, BL, BR. 137 The Granger Collection, MR; Culver Pictures Inc, B. 138 The Granger Collection, ML; Bettmann Archive, BR. 139 The Granger Collection, TL; Bettmann Archive, TR; Popperfoto, BL. 140 The Granger Collection, TL; Culver Pictures Inc, TR, Camera Press, B. 141 Bettmann Archive. 144 Camera Press, BL; Imperial War Museum, Dept of Photography, BR. 145 Culver Pictures Inc, TL; Imperial War Museum, Dept of Photography, TR. 146 The Granger Collection, BL; Culver Pictures Inc, BM. 147 Colorific. 148 Magnum Photos,

Robert Capa, BM; Bettmann Archives, BR. 149 Hulton-Deutsch; David King Collection, TR. 150 Magnum Photos, Henri Cartier Bresson. 151 Roger-Viollet, T; Robert Opie Collection, ML; Kobal Collection, MR; Hulton-Deutsch, B. 152 Popperfoto, TL; Martin Breese/Retrograph, ML; Kobal Collection, MR; Wiener Library, BL; Ullstein Bilderdienst, BR. 153 Hulton-Deutsch, T; Kobal Collection, M; Bettmann Archive/UPI, BL, BR. 154 Camera Press, T; Imperial War Museum, Dept of Photography, ML; Kobal Collection, MR; Imperial War Museum, Dept of Photography, B. 155 Popperfoto, TL, TR; Kobal Collection, ML; Camera Press, BR. 156 Bettmann Archive, T; David King Collection, ML; Kobal Collection, MR; Hulton-Deutsch, BL; Photography by Norman Brand, BR.

Front cover: Imperial War Museum, Dept of Photography, TL; Photography, Norman Brand (IWM, Dept of Exhibits & Firearms), TR, BL; Jean-Loup Charmet, ML; Hutlon-Deutsch, M; Imperial War Museum, Dept of Art, BM; Christine Vincent, BR.
Back cover: Photography, Norman Brand (IWM, Dept of Exhibits & Firearms), TL; Robert Opie Collection, TR; Robert Reynolds, M; The Robert Hunt Library, BL; Sovfoto, BR.

The editors are grateful to the following individuals and publishers for their kind permission to quote passages from the books below

Athlone Press Ltd from *Showa* by Tessa Morris- Suzuki 1984.
Jonathan Cape Ltd from *The People's War* by Angus Calder 1969.
Century Hutchinson from *Didn't You Know There's A War On?* by Jonathan Croall 1988.
Doubleday from *I Saw Tokyo Burning* by R Guillain 1981.
Grafton Books from *War Wives* by Colin and Eileen Townsend 1990.
Renata Greenshields from *Lucky Girl Goodbye* by Renata Greenshields 1988.
HarperCollins from *Naples '44* by Norman Lewis 1978.
Hill and Wang, and MacGibbon and Kee from *Night* by Elie Wiesel.
Macdonald Publishing Group from *Fighting for a Laugh* by Richard Fawkes.
Pantheon from *The Good War* by Studs Terkel 1984.
The Putnam Publishing Group from *The Home Front* by Harris, Michel and Schechter 1984.
Random House from *The Diary of Anne Frank* by Anne Frank 1952.
Scolar Press from *Raiders Overhead* by Barbara Nixon 1980.
Simon and Schuster from *The House Near Paris* by Drue Tartière 1946.
Time Life Books Inc from *The Resistance* by Russel Miller and the editors of Time Life Books 1979.
Viking from *Children of the Blitz* by Robert Westall 1985.
Wayland (Publishers) Ltd from *My Childhood in Nazi Germany* by Elsbeth Emrich 1991.